SPEAK OUT!
Debate and Public Speaking in the Middle Grades

☙❧

SPEAK OUT!

Debate and Public Speaking in the Middle Grades

⊂⊛⊃

Kate Shuster and John Meany

Published by

international debate education association

400 West 59th Street / New York, NY 10019

Library of Congress Cataloging-in-Publication Data

Shuster, Kate, 1974-
  Speak out! : debate and public speaking in the middle
grades / by Kate
Shuster and John Meany.
     p. cm.
   ISBN 1-932716-02-5 (pbk. : alk. paper)
  1. Debates and debating. 2. Public speaking. I. Meany,
John. II.
Title.
   PN4181.S53 2004
   808.5'3--dc22

Design by Hernan Bonomo
Printed in the USA

IDEBATE Press

Preface

Debate and public speaking are of extraordinary value to middle school students. Participation in debating can boost student self-confidence, accelerate learning across the curriculum, and improve critical thinking and oral communication skills.

This textbook supports the Middle School Public Debate Program (MSPDP), the largest and fastest growing middle school debate program in the world. The MSPDP is a unique program with a unique debate format. The format was designed in collaboration between college faculty and middle school teachers to maximize the rigor and accessibility of debating practice for all students in the middle grades.

The MSPDP began in 2002 as a pilot program in Southern California communities east of Los Angeles. In two years, it spread to more than sixty schools and now covers an area roughly the size of New England (minus Maine). In the first year of the program, almost 1,800 students participated in class and competitive debates. In the second year, the program nearly doubled in size. New MSPDP sites are now being established throughout the country.

Speak Out! is a primer for beginning and intermediate students participating in this program. Additional resources are available online at our support Web site, **www.middleschooldebate.com**. These include: a teacher's guide for the book; lesson plans, including plans for whole-class debating; and issue briefs to prepare students to debate dozens of current event topics.

We hope that this book simplifies teaching debate. The MSPDP is an empirically tested format that serves a wide range of students: the very gifted, those whose native language is not English, those not successful in traditional teaching situations, and even special education students. All the evidence we have collected as part of program evaluation over the first three years suggests that anyone, in any kind of community, within many kinds of constraints, can adopt the MSPDP program.

Should you wish to learn more about the program or provide the authors with feedback about the book, please email us at:

kate.shuster@claremontmckenna.edu or
john.meany@claremontmckenna.edu.

Acknowledgments

The authors gratefully and respectfully dedicate this book to all of the teachers, administrators, and students who have participated in the Middle School Public Debate Program in its first two years. The dozens of teachers with whom we have had the pleasure of working convinced us that some of our best and brightest citizens are currently teaching middle school. These teachers include Carly Huerta, Chad White, and Wally Lee, of Northview Intermediate in Duarte; Paul Bates, Dave Nygren, Sharyn MacCharles, and Melody Kohn, of Townsend Junior High in Chino Hills; Debbie Simon and Carol Lackpour of Canyon Hills Junior High in Chino Hills; Greg Paulk, Kelley Bieringer, and Jim Steir of Desert Springs Middle School in Desert Hot Springs; Kevin Summerfield of Coombs Middle School in Banning; Giovanna De La Paz of Nicolet Middle School in Banning; Anthony Gibson and Kennon Mitchell of Frisbie Middle School in Rialto; David Sawhill of Pioneer Middle School in Upland; Jennifer Davis of Van Avery Prep in Temecula; Diane Parker and Mike Sepulveda of Canyon Lake Middle School in Lake Elsinore; Manuel Peredia and Frank Robson of Mountain Shadows Middle School in Nuevo; Freda Kelly of Almeria Middle School in Fontana; Patricia Rynearson of Truman Middle School in Fontana; Beth Ferris of La Contenta Middle School in Yucca Valley; Ellen Hong of Campbell Hall in North Hollywood; Jesse Call of Pinacate Middle School in Perris; and Robert Tanous of Washington Middle School in Pasadena—all in California.

The many hundreds of students who have debated in class and competition as part of the MSPDP have shown us that brilliance is the norm for middle school students. We are indebted to all of these wonderful students for teaching us to think creatively about debate and argumentation.

Finally, we would like to extend a special thanks to Duarte community activist Jack Collins, without whom this project might never have been launched. He truly knows no peer in his dedication to learning.

Table of Contents

INTRODUCTION TO PUBLIC SPEAKING AND DEBATING

This section introduces you to basic and advanced techniques in public speaking and debating. You will also learn about the essential elements of the Middle School Public Debate Program (MSPDP) format. If you initially are uncomfortable about public speaking or are not sure you have the ability to speak and debate in public, you are in good company—most people are very nervous about public speaking. The best way to overcome this fear is to practice. With practice and dedication, you can become an accomplished speaker and debater.

CHAPTER 1:
INTRODUCTION TO PUBLIC SPEAKING

YOU communicate with others to share ideas and feelings, learn about the world, teach, develop self-confidence, participate in important decisions at school and in your community, and make friends. As you practice and increase your speaking and listening skills, you will pay closer attention to details; improve your class participation and get better grades; present your opinions in a convincing manner so that you can win the cooperation of others; and resolve conflicts without using name-calling, gossip, or violence. Good communication skills help you succeed in school and at work, improve your relationships with family and friends, and deal with challenges.

Public speaking skills help you meet new challenges. Effective public speakers are able to:

- Speak confidently with new people.
- Choose interesting subjects.
- Organize a speech that captures the audience's attention.
- Participate in serious discussions about school and community issues.
- Use language properly.
- Be more sensitive to the opinions of others.

You cannot just have the best idea; you cannot just have an entertaining presentation. Persuasive public speakers blend the right arguments with a clear and confident delivery. They are both entertaining and informative. They cleverly use many different kinds of effective public speaking **techniques**: organized and logical arguments, careful and proper use of words, simple and direct messages, powerful images, and interesting vocal delivery. Effective speakers research and know their topics, organize and practice their presentation, and anticipate their opponents' reactions.

There is no best way to deliver a speech; talented speakers use different techniques. Dr. Martin Luther King Jr., Winston Churchill, Cesar Chavez, Christiane Amanpour, Spike Lee, Hillary Clinton, Jerry Seinfeld, Rush Limbaugh, Dave Chappelle, Lesley Stahl, Michael Moore, and Oprah Winfrey do not deliver speeches in the same way. They adapt different speaking techniques to enhance their natural abilities. Their presentations are unique and consistently effective. The techniques they utilize may not be useful to others.

You learn public speaking just as you would any other new skill—identify your strengths and weaknesses, then work on improving your presentations through regular, patient practice. Speakers use many techniques to develop their skills and overcome nervousness or speech anxiety, but nothing works as well as practice.

This chapter introduces you to some of these techniques and provides practice tips to help you improve your public speaking.

VERBAL COMMUNICATION SKILLS

Your vocal delivery—how you present your speech—will influence how your audience hears your message. You cannot persuade another person of your opinion if you do not speak clearly and confidently.

But what does it mean to speak persuasively? How should you deliver a speech to convince someone?

Effective public speaking involves various elements:

- Volume
- Rate
- Emphasis
- Articulation
- Organization
- Word choice

VOLUME

You should deliver a speech at the appropriate volume. It should not be too soft—the audience should be able to hear it without straining. It should not be too loud—no one enjoys having a speaker YELL AN OPINION AT THEM! Deliver your speech in a slightly louder voice than you use in daily conversation. Additional volume shows that you are confident. Have you ever noticed the speaking styles used in TV commercials, by politicians and preachers, or on radio and TV talk shows? The speakers use volume to project confidence and win the agreement of their audience.

Speak more loudly in a large room than in a small one and in a more crowded room than in one with only a few people. You may raise and lower the volume of your delivery to emphasize an important point or show emotion. You might speak more loudly when you want to communicate anger or excitement. You might lower your voice to express grief, guilt, or concern. If you have been speaking in a conversational tone, raising your voice will get the audience's attention. Lowering your voice will force people to listen more closely.

To practice using volume, deliver a short section of a speech in different sized rooms and have a friend listen from the back. Is the speech loud enough for a classroom or larger area? Is it too loud for a small space?

RATE

The rate of delivery is the speed or pace of a speech. Some people speak too rapidly because they are nervous and want to finish quickly. Others speak too fast because their anxiety changes the way their body functions. A rapid heart rate and faster breathing may speed the pace of all actions, including speaking ("AndformyfirstpointIwouldliketo-discusstheissueofmysecondpointwhichis…").

On the other hand, some speakers deliver their messages too slowly. There are times when you want to speak slowly. Many effective speakers communicate their messages in a deliberate, planned, and careful way. If you present information that is new to the audience or difficult to understand, you would speak slowly so that they can pay careful attention. In addition, if you want to show the importance of an idea or event, you might speak slowly to emphasize a point. But, do not deliver a speech too slowly for the audience and the material involved.

You may have had the experience of knowing what a speaker was going to say before he completed his thought. Audiences find this type of delivery boring and frustrating. ("And so, in conclusion…we… should…remember…that our children…are…our…yes, it is important…to remember…that…our children…are…our…" Yes! Future! The word you need to finish that sentence is FUTURE! Say it! Say it!)

Your delivery should be slightly faster than your normal conversational speed, fast enough that the audience must pay attention. Your presentation will not be dull, and listeners will not fill in any words. They will not get distracted or daydream. Your pace will sound natural and keep their interest. They will understand the importance of your message and not lose track of key opinions or facts.

You can alter your rate of delivery by pausing. Speakers naturally pause at the conclusion of a sentence, in speech transitions (moving from one major part of a speech to another, or from one major argument to another), and at other points that emphasize key ideas.

Some pausing is effective. A brief pause after a rhetorical question (a question that you both ask and answer) encourages the audience to think about the question before you begin the answer. A pause just before key information allows listeners to concentrate on the importance of your message. You may pause after a dramatic or startling claim, giving the audience time to absorb the new information. If your opinions differ from what is expected, the audience will need time to think about your innovative ideas.

Repetition is also an effective form of pausing that calls attention to an important fact or opinion. Repeating the key parts of your speech reminds the audience that they should remember the point. Below is an example in which a speaker argues for the abolition of the death penalty.

> Twelve states have abolished the death penalty. In none of these has the homicide rate increased. (More slowly and clearly, enunciating each word.) No state that has abolished the death penalty has experienced an increase in homicides. (Now louder, and with more emphasis.) NOT ONE EXAMPLE!

Pauses can also change the pace of your speech and hurt your credibility. Avoid fillers ("you know, umm, whatever"). We use these vocalized pauses when we do not know what we are going to say next. Simply pause rather than use a vocalized pause. Here is how the example above would sound with vocalized pauses. If you say it aloud, you will realize immediately that the speech is not as effective as without the pauses.

> The, you know, death penalty has been, you know, abolished in twelve, umm, states, you know what I'm saying. In none, umm, of these states, umm, has the, you know, homicide rate increased...(More slowly and clearly, enunciating each word.) No, umm, state that has abolished, you know, the death penalty, or other stuff, has had an increase in, homicides, and whatever. (Now louder, and with more emphasis.) NOT ONE, YOU KNOW, EXAMPLE!

EMPHASIS

Do not emphasize all words equally. A good public speaker focuses the listener's attention on the specific words that have drama, substance, power, or imagery. She uses the pitch or tone of her voice to stress these key words.

Vocal tone or pitch matches the quality of the voice to the feeling of the speaker. For example, imagine two students examining their grades on a math test. One student tries hard but rarely gets a grade higher than a "C." The other is the top math student in the school; she always gets an "A." On this particular test, however, both students receive a "B." These students might use the same words in discussing their grades, but with a remarkably different tone. The first student would likely deliver the sentence "I got a 'B' on the math test" with some surprise and happiness in her voice. She would sound excited and hopeful. The second student's tone would indicate that she was not happy and suggest disappointment or worry. Both students used the same words, but they did not mean the same thing. The different tones mark the differences in the students' feelings.

Below are three statements. Can you imagine how you can give each more than one meaning through emphasis?

- I went to the principal's office.

- I think that I will be able to do it.

- This is the last time we will speak about this.

Speaking with the same tone quality for each syllable might be the way to present a speech in your robot voice ("Dan-ger-Will-Rob-in-son"), but it is not effective in persuading an audience. Good public speakers alter their tone to emphasize different feelings, attitudes, and meanings.

In some cases, you emphasize particular words not to express a feeling but to remind an audience of the important parts of an idea. If you delivered the following sentence, you might emphasize the underlined words.

The United States <u>federal government</u> should ensure that <u>each person</u> living in the country can afford quality <u>health care,</u>

In this case, you want your listeners to understand these points:

- The government is responsible for providing social services.

- Some social services should be universal—all people should have them.

- All people need health care.

A speaker's use of emphasis can bring emotion and attention to the important parts of an oral presentation.

SUGGESTED EXERCISES

Word and Phrase Emphasis

1. Read each sentence below to emphasize the desired meaning (in parenthesis).

   I already told you. (*Frustration*)

   I like you. (*Friendship*)

   Come back here. (*Anger*)

   You did that. (*Surprise*)

   I thought he would win. (*Irony*)

2. Read the following sentence several times, emphasizing a different word to achieve the quality in parenthesis.

   Mary is my friend. (*Agreement*)

   Mary is my friend. (*Pleasant surprise*)

   Mary is my friend. (*Shock or surprise*)

   Mary is my friend. (*Sarcasm*)

ARTICULATION

People pay close attention to what you say and how you say it when you speak in public. If you mispronounce a word, the audience probably will notice it. They might suspect that you do not know the subject or have not practiced your speech adequately. Mispronunciation can hurt your credibility. By focusing on articulation, you will pronounce words correctly and establish trust with the audience.

The English language is difficult; spelling is not always a reliable guide to pronunciation:

- Some letters have more than one pronunciation. (Compare the pronunciation of "**gh**" in the words "**gh**ost," "rou**gh**," "throu**gh**," and "ni**gh**t.")

- Some letters are not pronounced. (Examine the "h" in "hour," the "k" in "knife," and the "l" in "talk.")
- Different letters are used to produce the same sound. (Consider the "c" and the "s" in "censor" or "cereals.")

Spelling is tricky and can confuse pronunciation. You must develop your vocabulary and practice your speeches to deal with the challenges of proper pronunciation.

Articulation refers to the accurate pronunciation of words. An effective public speaker articulates a speech, saying each word the way a dictionary tells you to pronounce it.

The most common pronunciation errors occur when speakers use unfamiliar words. If you are delivering a speech on a new subject, learn the correct pronunciation of new words before using them. There is no excuse for mispronunciation! The easiest way to learn correct pronunciation is to use a dictionary. Repeat the word until you can say it easily. If you cannot find the correct pronunciation, substitute another word. Finally, use pronunciation exercises to reduce common errors and maintain your credibility.

WEB SITES FOR PRONUNCIATION

One Look Dictionary
www.onelook.com
More than 900 dictionaries are included in the Web search engine.

Merriam-Webster Online
www.m-w.com/home.htm
Webster's Dictionary and Thesaurus

You may also mispronounce words because the people around you pronounce them incorrectly, and you do not know that their pronunciation is wrong. Ask your teachers or experienced speakers to listen to your practice speeches for pronunciation errors. You can also study lists of commonly mispronounced words. Here are some examples:

COMMONLY MISPRONOUNCED WORDS

Correct pronunciation and spelling	Popular and incorrect pronunciation
Arctic (ark-tik)	Artic (ar-tik)
formerly (for-mer-lee)	formally (for-mal-lee)
library (lie-brer-ee)	libary (lie-bar-ee)
nuclear (noo-klee-ar)	nucular (noo-kew-lar)
suppose (su-poz)	susppose (sus-poz)
picture (pik-chur)	piture (pit-chur)
tyranny (tear-an-ee))	tyranny (tie-ran-ee)

On some occasions, careless pronunciation leads to an error. This problem is as common as not knowing the correct pronunciation. You must practice pronouncing sounds and words clearly to avoid errors. Often, we become careless in casual or conversational speech, forgetting to open our mouths and move our lips and tongues as we should. This slurred or sloppy speech reduces the effectiveness of a presentation and makes it very difficult to understand.

One type of pronunciation error stems from dropping the ends of words. For example, "stopped" becomes "stop" or "escaping" becomes "escape." At other times, casual speakers substitute softer sounds for sharper ones because a softer sound requires less mouth muscle movement. In these cases, a word like "later" sounds more like "ladder," because it takes less energy to make a "d" sound than it does a "t" sound. To speak well, you must open your mouth, avoid mumbling, and move your tongue and your lips fully. This requires practice.

Techniques to improve pronunciation require you to articulate unusual or difficult words and phrases. They force you to concentrate on each sound, helping you to eliminate casual speaking errors. Practice difficult individual sounds, tongue twisters, and unfamiliar quotations or speeches to develop your pronunciation. You also can use these exercises to practice volume, rate of delivery, emphasis, and other public speaking skills.

Using proper pronunciation does not mean that you must speak without an accent. After all, everyone has an accent, even if it is from a particular region of a country. For example, although native English speakers from Boston and Atlanta use the same language, they have distinct regional accents. People from Atlanta can easily identify a visitor from Boston, based solely on the accent. Pronunciation is a general guide to the correct way to say a word, and speakers can pronounce correctly even with their natural accents.

SUGGESTED EXERCISES

Letter Groups

Slowly repeat each of the following letter groups:

- www, www, www, www, wdw, wdw, www, www, www, wtw, wtw, wtw
- lll, lll, lwl, lwl, lll, lll, ltl, ltl, lkl, lkl, lll, lll, lwl, lwl, lhl, lhl, ltl, ltl, lkl, lkl, lwl
- www, bbb, ddd, www, kgh, ddd, www, kgh, lwl, www, wdw, lwl, wbw, www

Tongue Twisters

Speaking at a conversational or slightly faster rate of delivery, repeat each of the following tongue twisters three or four times.

- Six sick slick slim sycamore saplings
- Three free throws
- Unique New York
- Toy boat. Toy boat. Toy boat.
- Mrs. Smith's Fish Sauce Shop
- Lovely lemon liniment
- Black bug's blood
- Preshrunk silk shirts
- Flash message!
- Are our oars oak?

Similarities

Articulate each pair of similarly sounding words. Make sure that a listener can hear the difference clearly.

ball	bald	late	lake
bog	bug	look	luck
bus	boss	made	mad
climb	crime	met	mat
dad	dab	not	note

eat	it	ran	run
berry	very	run	rung
fond	found	said	sad
get	got	they	day
just	jest	wake	wade

Quotations from Shakespeare

One way to improve public speaking is to practice speeches that contain unfamiliar words and phrases. William Shakespeare wrote the speech below four centuries ago, and so the language may seem foreign to you. That's the point. Speaking unfamiliar and unusual words forces you to concentrate on each word and sentence. Read this excerpt from *Macbeth* quietly, then deliver the speech aloud two or three times, practicing pronunciation, volume, pace, and clarity.

"'Tomorrow' Speech"

Macbeth's plan to become the ruler of Scotland by assassination has failed. He is under attack at his castle. He realizes that his scheming has achieved nothing and that he has lost everything. He is disgusted by his failure and knows that his end is near.

Tomorrow, and tomorrow, and tomorrow
Creeps in this petty pace from day to day,
To the last syllable of recorded time;
And all our yesterdays have lighted fools
The way to dusty death. Out, out brief candle!
Life's but a walking shadow, a poor player
That struts and frets his hour upon the stage
And then is heard no more: it is a tale
Told by an idiot, full of sound and fury,
Signifying nothing.

My Speech

Introduction

Main Body

Conclusion

ORGANIZATION

To debate successfully, you must do far more than pronounce words properly. You use words to deliver a message, offer an opinion, share your knowledge, and persuade others. To succeed in debate, you must express your ideas effectively. The message should be simple, direct, and clear.

An effective speech should:

- Follow a simple structure
- Have a logical sequence of ideas.

Most people are familiar with simple narrative structure; it is the order in which a story is told. This structure has three parts: an introduction, a main body, and a conclusion. It provides a clear outline for the design and delivery of effective speeches.

INTRODUCTION

Begin your speech with a brief introduction, letting the audience know: Who? What? and Why?

Who are you?

Identify yourself to the audience. Think of public speaking as meeting someone for the first time. When you meet a person, you greet them by telling them your name and who you are. The same is true for public speaking. The introduction is an opportunity for you to greet the audience.

What are you speaking about?

Audiences expect you to tell them the topic and theme of your speech. The introduction is a preview of your speech. It alerts the audience to what they should listen for and learn from your presentation.

Why should they listen to you?

The audience wants to know what new information you have to offer. Your introduction should include an attention-getter, some information or dramatic use of a public speaking skill that lets the audience know why they should listen. You might open your speech with energy, intensity, and a sense of drama; or you might use humor to entertain the audience. Clever ideas or surprising facts will convince them that you have information from which they can benefit.

MAIN BODY

The main body of the speech is the heart of your presentation. You should make two or three major points, any one of which would prove that you are correct about the issue at hand. Each major point should be well reasoned and supported with appropriate evidence. (The evidence might be in the form of statistics, historical or contemporary examples, or the opinions of experts.)

You should explain each of the major points of a speech in a logical order. You can organize ideas chronologically (How did the events occur in time? Which came first? Which was second? Which was last?); by cause and effect (How did that action lead to that result?); or based on a problem and solution (What is the ongoing problem? What can we do to put an end to it?). The logical sequencing of ideas makes a speech easy to follow.

CONCLUSION

Finally, you should have a compelling and powerful conclusion that reminds the audience of the main points of your speech. It should include a short sentence that summarizes the purpose of your presentation. ("Peer pressure has its good side." "He really proved that this country would be better off with a lower voting age." "Yes, it is a better idea to improve city life than build more gated neighborhoods in the suburbs.")

WORD CHOICE

An effective public speaker carefully selects the appropriate words to convey her message most accurately and persuasively. Is a meal that you thoroughly enjoyed "good" or "delicious"? Is the new videogame "fun" or "exciting"? Was the Holocaust "bad" or "horrific"? If you want to persuade others or make meaningful distinctions in what you say, you need to use vivid, powerful images to describe your ideas. Your words matter. Listeners are affected by your choice of language. Strong wording will always make your arguments more credible.

PERSUASIVE WORDS

abolish	duty	more	resist
act	easily	move	restore
adopt	eliminate	natural	revolutionary
avoid	ensure	overcome	save
awesome	focus	patriotism	security
best	forward	plan	sensational
better	freedom	policy	simple
breakthrough	guarantee	powerful	simplify
capture	identity	prepare	solve
change	implement	prevent	superior
collapse	improve	progress	tradition
compare	innovate	protection	triumph
connect	justice	quickly	truth
crisis	liberty	recommended	ultimate
deliver	lifesaving	remove	understand
deny	manage	replace	urgent
discover	mobilize	responsibility	use

PHRASES TO CONVINCE

already successful	longer lasting
as the evidence shows	move forward
at last	new method
bold new step	now is the time
call to action	on the brink
for example	pilot program
high quality	problem free
important development	take steps
in this case	the fact of the matter is
it's now or never	the key to
last chance	the truth is

Word your claims strongly and authoritatively. Audiences will appreciate and remember your message if it is strongly worded. Do not exaggerate! If you word your claims more strongly than necessary, the audience might think you are untrustworthy or that you do not know your facts. You may lose their attention or confidence. This result is as bad as using imprecise or weak words.

While effective words and phrases can strengthen your speech, ineffective words can hurt it. Good public speakers avoid words and phrases that create fear or concern, or are too simplistic or vague.

SOME WORDS AND PHRASES TO AVOID		
bad	like	very
cost	nervous	whatever
difficult	really	worry
good	stuff	you know
hard	things	

Always avoid prejudice and stereotypes in your language. Racist and sexist speech, unnecessarily violent or hostile images, and the use of offensive language will destroy your credibility, and your audience will miss or ignore your effective points.

NONVERBAL COMMUNICATION SKILLS

Nonverbal communication is an important part of a persuasive delivery. You use nonverbal communication, often called "body language," daily. Nods, smiles, shrugs, frowns, gestures, and other body movements send powerful signals from you to others.

Nonverbal communication can refer to the position of a person in a room (in the center or to the side, in the front or the back), facial expressions, eye contact, posture, use of gestures, body movement, and dress. Nonverbal techniques can communicate a lot about you and your message. You can show your emotions, identify the differences and points of agreement you have with the audience or other speakers, and emphasize the important issues in your speech.

Public speakers must develop their nonverbal communication skills to make their presentations consistent and effective. Nonverbal messages can contradict verbal ones. Unless you are aware of your nonverbal communication, you may sabotage your speech.

The major elements of nonverbal communication for successful public speaking include:

- Body positioning and movement
- Eye contact

- Gestures

- Poise

BODY POSITIONING AND MOVEMENT

Effective public speakers establish a line-of-sight with the audience. They use their body position, posture, and movement to attract and hold the attention of their listeners. You should stand front and center in a room, unless another location makes it easier for the audience to see you. If you are using a lectern, podium, or platform, make sure that you do not stand behind it for your entire speech. Effective speakers are not "talking heads," barely visible above a piece of furniture.

Position yourself in the center of the room, but feel confident enough to move (just a small movement; avoid pacing around the room) to the side of a lectern or desk to deliver a section of the speech. The movement will provide a welcome break for listeners, who will quickly tire of watching you deliver an entire speech from one spot. Imagine a television show, videogame, or movie in which a person stands in only one spot while speaking to the camera. Would you be excited about watching it? Your audience will not pay attention to you unless you consider appropriate body movement.

If you cannot move from one spot because of space constraints or technical limitations (for example, you may have to use an immovable microphone), you can use eye contact and nonverbal messages to influence the audience.

Before you begin your presentation, determine your starting spot, the place in the room from which you will speak. Good posture is important. Stand with your feet firmly on the floor, your weight evenly balanced, and your knees slightly bent. Pull your shoulders up and back, and lift your head. This is a comfortable and confident pose. If your weight is balanced, you will not shift from side to side or rock back and forth, which distracts the audience.

TO BEGIN A SPEECH

- Wait until the audience is ready.
- Make eye contact.
- Relax with a deep breath.
- Be enthusiastic.

Wait until the audience is ready for you to begin. Look directly at them as you start your introduction. You might even lean forward slightly or take a small step forward. This helps you connect with the audience. Avoid looking down at your notes or away from the audience. These actions are like looking at the ground when you shake hands for the first time—they show shyness or awkwardness. They are not inviting, and you need to welcome the audience to your speech.

Stand still as you deliver your introduction and try to look relaxed. After you have established a confident presence, you should move a few feet to a new position. This allows audience members who may not have had a good view of you during your introduction to see you more easily. This movement also attracts the audience's attention. You must remind the audience, with nonverbal communication as well as with your voice, that they should pay attention. Movement helps do this.

EYE CONTACT

Eye contact is valuable, even if you are able to move throughout a room. People first learn communication through eye contact (when you were a baby, your parents held you close when speaking to you). The members of an audience will expect a similar kind of communication—a personal touch—even if you are not standing or sitting next to them. Eye contact reaches out to an audience and pulls them in. It bridges the physical distance between the speaker and her listeners.

EYE CONTACT

Many public speakers do not use eye contact because they are anxious or embarrassed. Others rely too heavily on their notes and make the mistake of reading their speech. Some stop using eye contact when they talk about serious or painful topics.

Eye contact is important for the speaker's credibility. It connects him to the audience and establishes trust. Eye contact can personalize a speech. You may not be able to look at every person in a crowded room but you should look in each direction. This lets your listeners know that your message is for them, not just for those directly in front of you.

When they are first giving oral presentations, many students do not know what to do with their hands. Should they clasp them together and place them behind their back? Should they hold on to the side of the lecturn? Should they use one hand to hold their notes? Should they raise their arms in victory for the entire speech?

You can do many of these things (except raising your hands in victory!), but remember not to hold your hands in one position for too long. Using gestures adds movement to your presentation and helps you emphasize important points. Controlling gestures is an important skill for an effective speaker.

Gestures include hand movements, which you might use to stress an important word or idea. Plan your gestures in advance and use them in a well thought out, organized way to support key features of your speech.

You might, for example, point at the audience if you want to stress their responsibility to think or do something. A flick of your hand outward with palm down works well when you are saying negative words like "not" or "none." You can use this gesture to dismiss your opponents' ideas and show that the audience agrees with your opinion of the opposition's point.

You can use gestures to help the audience visualize your message. If you are describing how little effort schools make in helping poor students succeed, you might place your thumb and forefinger together, or hold your palm out and slowly lower it toward the floor. Either of these gestures indicates a small and/or decreasing amount. Both would help the audience understand your point about shrinking support for student achievement.

Other common gestures can help the audience follow your organization. For example, you might count on your fingers when you give an overview of the "three major points" you will cover. You might open your arms to embrace the opinions of the audience. You might gesture very slightly in the air to punctuate the final words of your conclusion. (For example, each of these words might get a quick and subtle gesture as you powerfully and carefully announce: "Now…is…the…time… to…act!")

If you must deliver your speech from behind a podium, keep your gestures above or to the side of the furniture or else the audience will not see them. If you are not using a lectern, gesture within the frame of your body. Movement that is far from your body makes you appear out of control.

There are other points to remember when using gestures:

- **Do not point at the audience too frequently.** The audience perceives this gesture as disrespectful and aggressive. (No one likes to have a finger jabbing at them.)

- **Do not hold anything in your hand.** Holding a pen or a similar object can be distracting. The audience will follow it like an orchestra following a conductor's baton or a dog chasing a bone.

- **Avoid putting your hands in your pockets.** People often associate this gesture with being sneaky, and if you have keys, coins, or anything that makes noise, the movement will distract the audience.

- **Avoid gestures that are too simple or repetitive.** Do not hold up a finger signaling one for your first point, two fingers for two, an additional third finger for three, and so on. It is better to say, "My first point will be… ," and save your gestures for more complex parts of your speech that might need nonverbal support.

- **Avoid constantly moving your hands and arms.** Gestures are appropriate, but like your possessions, you should take them out, use them, and put them away when you are finished. Return to a comfortable standing position, with your hands at your side or held in front or behind you for major portions of your speech. Flapping arms, opening and closing hands, and constant motion distract the audience and make it easy for them to miss your message.

Facial expressions and head movements, such as smiles and nods or shaking the head to show disagreement, are effective gestures that add to a speaker's credibility. Do not smile while presenting a serious subject. Smiling while discussing human rights violations or war crimes will make the audience think that you do not take your speech seriously or that there is something wrong with you. Your facial expressions should match the subject. They should support the emotion or attitude you would like to convey. You should be pleasant, professional, and formal, but there are occasions for passion, drama, and anger. The audience will better understand your message when your nonverbal communication and spoken words work together to express your ideas.

POISE

The best public speakers have poise. When a speaker has poise, he displays confidence, dignity, and professional conduct. Poise is often associated with leadership ability. Poise is the quality of being in control, having direction and motivation, and staying focused on the task at hand. In other words, a speaker who acts in a respectful and responsible manner has poise. This speaker will not overreact to the issue, the audience, or any opposing voice. The poised speaker shows self-confidence but is never arrogant. In a debate, a poised speaker will be a gracious winner and an honorable loser.

Rehearse the nonverbal portions of your presentation just as you would the verbal parts of your speech. Practice positioning, movement, eye contact, gestures, and poise. This will help you remember how and when to use appropriate nonverbal techniques.

SPEECH ANXIETY

Public speaking is one of people's primary fears, sometimes ranked ahead of death. Many people try to avoid speaking in public or experience significant anxiety before they do so. You may feel dizzy, have a dry mouth, sweaty palms, a racing pulse, or even begin to shake. These are normal reactions, but anxiety can be identified and managed—even reduced. Eliminate caffeine before delivering a speech. Light exercise earlier in the day will help relax muscles and reduce tension. Most importantly, use breathing techniques before and during your presentation.

Breath control enables you to speak forcefully and clearly. In addition, proper breathing helps you cope with nervousness and relax during a presentation. Before delivering your speech, do some deep breathing. Inhale deeply through your nose for a count of three, hold your breath for a count of three, exhale through your mouth for a count of three, and hold your breath again for a count of three. Repeat the exercise two more times. This deep breathing exercise will help you relax.

You will also need breath control during your speech so that you do not get nervous and speak too quickly. To breathe properly during the speech, practice some of the exercises below.

SUGGESTED EXERCISES

Breathing Exercises: Lists

Inhale normally and comfortably. Speak each of the numbers in item "A" in a clear and confident voice, pronouncing each with a single breath. Repeat this exercise using the other three lists. Once you can speak each of these lists in a strong and persuasive manner, combine "A" and "B" and speak all twenty numbers in a single breath. Next, practice a combination of "C" and "D."

A. 1-2-3-4-5-6-7-8-9-10

B. 11-12-13-14-15-16-17-18-19-20

C. A-B-C-D-E-F-G-H-I-J-K

D. L-M-N-O-P-Q-R-S-T-U-V-W-X-Y-Z

Breathing Exercises: Quotations

Say each of the following sentences on a single breath. Remember to speak clearly, with sufficient volume. (You might also memorize some of these quotations to use in your speeches.)

- It could probably be shown by facts and figures that there is no distinctly American criminal class except Congress. *Mark Twain*

- Suppose you were an idiot and suppose you were a member of Congress. But I repeat myself. *Mark Twain*

- This country has come to feel the same when Congress is in session as when the baby gets hold of a hammer. *Will Rogers*

- If all economists were laid end to end, they would not reach a conclusion. *George Bernard Shaw*

- Economics is extremely useful as a form of employment for economists. *John Kenneth Galbraith*

- If the facts don't fit the theory, change the facts. *Albert Einstein*

- For every action there is an equal and opposite government program. *Bob Wells*

- Anyone who is capable of getting themselves made President should on no account be allowed to do the job. *Douglas Adams*

- All truth passes through three stages. First, it is ridiculed. Second, it is violently opposed. Third, it is accepted as being self-evident. *Arthur Schopenhauer*

- The public will believe anything, so long as it is not founded on truth. *Edith Sitwell*

- If liberty and equality, as is thought by some are chiefly to be found in democracy, they will be best attained when all persons alike share in the government to the utmost. *Aristotle*

- All animals are equal but some animals are more equal than others. *George Orwell*

- The mystery of government is not how Washington works but how to make it stop. *P. J. O'Rourke*

- Ancient Rome declined because it had a Senate; now what's going to happen to us with both a Senate and a House? *Will Rogers*

- Even if you're on the right track, you'll get run over if you just sit there. *Will Rogers*
- Freedom is not worth having if it does not include the freedom to make mistakes. *Mahatma Gandhi*
- What difference does it make to the dead, the orphans and the homeless, whether the mad destruction is wrought under the name of totalitarianism or the holy name of liberty or democracy? *Mahatma Gandhi*
- The difference between the right word and the almost right word is the difference between lightning and a lightning bug. *Mark Twain*

FINAL TIPS FOR PUBLIC SPEAKING

Proper preparation will help reduce speech anxiety.

- **Set realistic goals.** Identify the purpose of the speech and what you must do to make it effective. You do not have to deliver the best speech ever; make an effective speech for the moment.

- **Know your material.** Research the topic and understand the information. If you are secure about the information, your confidence will carry over to your performance.

- **Speak extemporaneously and not from memory.** If you memorize your speech, you might forget part of it. Understand the information and speak from limited notes. If you know the material, an outline should be sufficient. For example, if someone asks you a question about your family, your school, or your favorite music, you would not need notes to answer them because you know the information well. You might, however, need brief notes to deliver an organized presentation on these subjects. If you understand the material for your speech in the same way, you might need notes to follow the organization of your presentation, but you will not need a full written or memorized speech. You should be able to talk about the issue in a natural way.

- **Have a positive attitude.** Think positively about yourself, and you will deliver your speech with confidence. Visualize presenting your speech effectively. Finally, audiences usually are very supportive of speakers. Do not worry if they will like you. Remember, most people fear public speaking and so they think highly of anyone who attempts it.

- **Practice! Practice! Practice!**

LISTENING

Finding a public-speaking role model will help your practice. You may know family, friends, teachers, and neighbors who are confident public speakers. Focus on their style of delivery and the content of their message. Effective speakers appeal to you because they have something important to say and the ability to say it in an interesting way. Study how they present their message so you can discover techniques you can use. You will also identify important details about people, places, and current events that will make your speeches more informative and exciting.

Listen to people you like. What voice qualities do they have? Listen to people that you do not like. Do they speak in a way that is irritating or annoying? What voice qualities are unpleasant? Listen to several reporters on local television news stations (for example, a person delivering the news, another talking about sports, and another discussing the weather). How do they speak when they present serious information? Is it different from the way they speak to other people on the broadcast, such as another newscaster, the sportscaster, or the weather reporter? Can you tell just from the tone of their voice if they are discussing a serious or a not-so-serious story?

SUGGESTED EXERCISES

Great Speeches

Read the following speech silently. If you do not understand some of the words used in the speech, consult the vocabulary list. Then, have another student read the speech to you. Answer the questions below.

> The preamble of the federal Constitution says: "We, the people of the United States, in order to form a more perfect union, establish justice, insure domestic tranquility, provide for the common defense, promote the general welfare, and secure the blessings of liberty to ourselves and our posterity, do ordain and establish this Constitution for the United States of America." It was we, the people; not we, the white male citizens; nor yet we, the male citizens; but we, the whole people, who formed the Union. And we formed it, not to give the blessings of liberty, but to secure them; not to the half of ourselves and the half of our posterity, but to the whole people—

women as well as men. And it is a downright mockery to talk to women of their enjoyment of the blessings of liberty while they are denied the use of the only means of securing them provided by this democratic-republican government—the ballot. For any state to make sex a qualification that must ever result in the disfranchisement of one entire half of the people is to pass a bill of attainder, or an ex post facto law, and is therefore a violation of the supreme law of the land. By it the blessings of liberty are forever withheld from women and their female posterity. To them this government has no just powers derived from the consent of the governed. To them this government is not a democracy. It is not a republic. It is an odious aristocracy; a hateful oligarchy of sex; the most hateful aristocracy ever established on the face of the globe; an oligarchy of wealth, where the rich govern the poor. An oligarchy of learning, where the educated govern the ignorant, or even an oligarchy of race, where the Saxon rules the African, might be endured; but this oligarchy of sex, which makes father, brothers, husband, sons, the oligarchs over the mother and sisters, the wife and daughters of every household—which ordains all men sovereigns, all women subjects, carries dissension, discord and rebellion into every home of the nation. Webster, Worcester and Bouvier all define a citizen to be a person in the United States, entitled to vote and hold office. The only question left to be settled now is: Are women persons? And I hardly believe any of our opponents will have the hardihood to say they are not. Being persons, then, women are citizens; and no state has a right to make any law, or to enforce any old law, that shall abridge their privileges or immunities. Hence, every discrimination against women in the constitutions and laws of the several states is today null and void, precisely as in every one against Negroes.

Susan B. Anthony
Are Women Persons?
(1873)

VOCABULARY WORDS

preamble		the introduction of a speech or written document
tranquility		peace
posterity		future generations of people
ordain		formally create by law
Union		a reference to the United States
mockery		making something or someone look ridiculous
securing		guaranteeing
democratic-republican		democracy in which the people elect the head of state and the government
disenfranchisement		to deprive or take away a right or privilege, in this case, the right to vote
bill of attainder		finding that someone is guilty of treason or a felony without a trial
ex post facto		Latin for "after the fact"; for example, a law that punishes people for behavior that was legal when the action was performed
derived		to get something from
consent		agreement
republic		a form of government in which the people vote for the individuals who govern them
odious		leading to hatred and disgust
aristocracy		a government ruled by a privileged class
oligarchy		a government controlled by a small group of people
sovereigns		rulers
subjects		persons under the rule or control of another
dissension		disagreement or difference of opinion
discord		strong, perhaps even violent, disagreement
Webster, Worcester and Bouvier		popular dictionaries
entitled		a right to receive something
hardihood		being tough or brave
abridge		deprive somebody of their rights
privileges		advantages, rights, or benefits
immunities		a protection against harm
null and void		amounts to nothing; for a law, it means that the law has no effect

Discussion questions:

- What is the author's main argument?
- Do you think that her argument is effective? Why?
- Is there anything in her speech that hurts her argument?

Current Event

This exercise will prepare you to:

- Listen to a report on an important current event
- Identify major argument points
- Take careful notes.

Ask another student or a debate partner to read a major news story to you. Listen carefully. Take notes and write, in order, each of the major points. Now read your notes to the person who read you the story. Did you miss any major points? Repeat the exercise. Is the story easier to understand the second time? Did you have better notes?

Now try the exercise with a different newspaper or magazine article. Although it is a different story, was it easier to take notes this time? Change places with your partner and read other stories to him for his listening practice.

Debate Speech

A speaker is making a case to prove the topic "The death penalty should be abolished." Have another student read the speech aloud to you. Listen and take careful notes, as if you were going to answer the main arguments.

Justice should include mercy and forgiveness, but the death penalty in the United States is not only unforgiving, it is also unfair. Although some believe that it provides justice for the worst sorts of crimes, in practice it does not work. Racial minorities, the poor, the mentally ill, and the retarded are more likely to receive a death sentence than other segments of the population. Even innocent people have received death sentences!

In Illinois, more than half of 300 death sentences were reversed or reduced on appeal. It is troubling that a person might be executed for a crime that he or she did not commit. Not only would the wrong person be executed, but also the real killer would still be free, perhaps threatening other innocent people. The danger that innocent people will be executed is increasing. Many people on death row were convicted and sentenced more than ten years ago, before the introduction of DNA and other sophisticated forensic tests in criminal trials. These inmates may be able to prove their innocence with modern scientific testing but do not have the money or other support to investigate their cases.

The death penalty does not deter murder and other crimes. According to the FBI's Preliminary Uniform Crime Report for 2002, the murder rate in the South increased by 2.1 percent from 2001, while the murder rate in the Northeast decreased by almost 5 percent. The South accounts for 82 percent of all executions since 1976; the Northeast accounts for less than 1 percent. The California Paralegal's Association also reported that four new studies threw further doubt on the deterrent effect of the death penalty. In addition, abolition of the death penalty has not led to an increase in murder. The homicide rate has not increased in the twelve U.S. states that have abandoned it.

The United States might lose its moral and political leadership in the world because of its use of the death penalty. Most U.S. allies have abolished capital punishment. Canada, Mexico, and most of Central and South America have eliminated it as has Western Europe. Russia commuted the death sentence for all 700 inmates on death row. More than 100 countries have abolished the death penalty. Many countries are also concerned about how the United States applies the death penalty. There is an international ban on executing juvenile offenders and the mentally retarded, but the United States leads the world in executing juvenile inmates. Texas alone executed seven inmates under the age of eighteen. The United States also regularly executed the mentally retarded; twenty-six states permitted it until a recent Supreme Court decision prohibited the practice. The world increasingly views the United States as violating international law and human rights because it executes its citizens and the citizens of other countries. The death penalty is immoral and ought to be abolished.

Discussion questions:

1. The speaker opposes the death penalty. What are his major argments for abolishing it?

2. Does the speaker have evidence for each of the major points? What kind of evidence does the speaker provide?

3. How is the United States affected internationally because of its use of the death penalty?

4. Does the majority of the world's nations support the death penalty?

5. Does the death penalty stop murder and other serious crimes?

6. Name two reasons to support the death penalty that are not part of the speech.

CHAPTER 2:
INTRODUCTION TO DEBATING

THERE are many different ways to debate. This book focuses on the Middle School Public Debate Program (MSPDP) format. It is a modified version of parliamentary debating, the most popular debate format in the world. The MSPDP format was designed specifically for students in the middle grades, although those younger or older also can benefit from it.

Parliamentary debate is used in primary school, middle school, high school, and college classes, and in debating contests in more than forty countries. The MSPDP model is the primary format for middle-school debating in the United States. As you learn to debate in this format, you will join a growing international community of students who are seriously committed to developing advanced argumentation and persuasive speaking skills.

This chapter explains the rules, popular practices, and recommended strategies for successfully debating in the MSPDP format. In addition, it shows what each speaker tries to accomplish in her speech. Each speaker has an important role in the debate. To succeed, she must complete the tasks that are part of her debate assignment. These are known as the speaker duties or speaker responsibilities. In addition to making her own speech, each person is part of a team. It takes effective teamwork to win debates consistently. We also show how each debater should work with the other members of her team to prepare for, and succeed in, debate competitions.

As you begin examining MSPDP debating, you will notice that there are few rules. Debating is an open event. The very nature of debate encourages students to be creative. Too many rules might interfere with the development of innovative ideas and strategies.

Because there are only a few basic rules, new participants can begin debating immediately. Nevertheless, debating can be a difficult skill to master. Many participants discover new things as they go from middle-school to high-school to college-level debating. In fact, one of the joys of debating is learning that there is always more to learn. You will grow intellectually, no matter how many debates you have had, no matter how much experience you gain. Having limited rules enables new students to participate in serious debates immediately while freeing advanced students to learn sophisticated techniques and new strategies.

A GENERAL UNDERSTANDING OF DEBATING

What is a debate? A debate is an organized public argument on a specific topic. It is organized, in that there are rules of debating. It is public because it is conducted for the benefit of an audience. It involves arguments, which are well-explained opinions. A debate is also on a specific topic, with one side arguing in favor and the other team opposing the issue.

Debaters have a specific definition of argument that differs from what we use in daily life. Many people define a conflict with friends, family, or co-workers as an argument. For example, a disagreement with your brother or sister over who is responsible for completing a household chore might proceed like this:

You: I cleaned the kitchen floor last time.

Your brother: No, you didn't.

You: Yes, I did.

Your brother: No, you didn't.

You: Yes, I did! I did it last time.

Your brother: Wrong! I did it last time.

You: That's not true. I cleaned it last time.

Some say that popular television programs, such as *The Jerry Springer Show*, involve people in public arguments. These kinds of programs have guests engaged in arguments like this:

Guest 1: You didn't treat me fairly.

Guest 2: Yes I did.

Guest 1: No, you were never fair.

Guest 2: I always treat you right.

Guest 1: No, you don't.

Guest 2: Yes, I do.

Guest 1: You don't know me.

Guest 2: You don't know ME!

In these cases, the participants are involved in a discussion that includes conflict, passion, disagreement, misunderstanding, and loud, angry voices. Debate arguments, however, use reasoning and evidence to support opinion. In each of the examples above, the participants disagree but never fully explain their opinions, nor do they offer evidence to support their ideas. When was the kitchen floor last cleaned? Is there any proof that either person recently cleaned the floor? How was the first guest treated unfairly? In what way was the guest mistreated? Or was the guest ever treated badly? Is there any proof supporting the opinion of either guest, for example, an eyewitness to mistreatment or a witness who could show that the second guest was an honorable and fair person? Although we often call these kinds of conflicts arguments, they do not meet the definition of argument used in debate. In a debate, an argument is an opinion supported by reasoning and evidence.

Popular conflicts and misunderstandings are not like formal debates in other ways. For example, common disagreements are not organized. They have no rules. There is no speaking order or time allotted to each speaker. One speaker may try to shout down another. The discussion is for the benefit of the people involved in the misunderstanding, while in a debate it is for the benefit of a third party—a judge or audience. Finally, a common disagreement may involve more than one topic. The discussion might start with complaints about cleaning the kitchen floor and quickly move to borrowed CDs, loans, and other personal complaints. In a formal debate, the individuals and teams stick to the topic.

DEBATING IS LIKE A TRIAL

Parliamentary debate in the MSPDP format is similar to arguments made in a court before a jury. There are two sides in a U.S. criminal trial: the prosecution and the defense. The prosecution argues that a particular person is guilty of a crime. This is called making a case. The lawyer for the prosecution, also known as a district attorney, must make a very specific case. She must prove that the defendant, John Doe, is responsible for violating a specific law. The prosecutor has a topic to prove: John Doe committed a particular illegal act. She must present evidence that proves John Doe is a criminal. The evidence may include eyewitnesses, the defendant's confession, videotapes of the defendant committing the crime, and other physical or circumstantial evidence, such as stolen property found in the defendant's home. She must organize her arguments and present her evidence in a way that convinces the jury that John Doe is guilty beyond a reasonable doubt.

John Doe has his own lawyer at the trial. The defense counsel will argue against the case for the prosecution. He might try to prove that the prosecutor is wrong, arguing that the facts do not support her case. He might also argue that there is an innocent explanation for John Doe's behavior or try to prove that another person was responsible for the crime. He might use other strategies, but he has one mission: to demonstrate that the prosecution failed to prove its case beyond a reasonable doubt.

At the end of the trial, the case goes to a jury, which is the finder of fact. It listens to the lawyers, considers testimony, and examines the evidence that both sides have presented. After careful deliberation, the jurors reach a decision. If the prosecution has proved its case, the jury will find the defendant guilty; if the defense can show reasonable doubt, it will acquit him.

Parliamentary debate in the United States is loosely based on this model. In a general sense, parliamentary debate follows the argumentation manner in a modern courtroom. Just as in the example above, there are two sides in a debate. Instead of being named the prosecution and the defense, the sides are called the proposition and the opposition. The proposition team has the same job as the prosecution lawyer: to prove a case. The opposition team has the same job as the defense counsel. It must show that the proposition's case is wrong. In debates, the proposition team has the burden of proving their case; however, this proof does not normally have to be beyond a reasonable doubt, as it would in a criminal trial. In a trial, the jury is usually the finder of fact. It makes the decision about guilt or innocence. It determines whether the prosecution or the defense has the better argument. In

A DEBATE IS LIKE A TRIAL

- It has a narrow topic
- It has two sides
- Both sides use evidence
- There is a judge or jury
- One side has the burden of proof

a debate, a judge functions as the jury. She is the finder of fact and decides whether the proposition or opposition has won.

A trial, like most organized discussions, begins with a topic. A topic is a focused set of ideas used to direct a discussion to a specific subject. In a trial, the prosecution has a topic: the defendant's alleged crime. That's it. The discussion must focus on the defendant's responsibility for a particular crime. If the defendant is a mean person, or his children do not get along with him, or he does not vote, or he does not make an effort to be friendly to neighbors, you might not want to know or be friends with him. None of this information, however, is relevant to the case. For the prosecution lawyer, the topic might be "John Doe committed a robbery of $200 or more from the First Street Supermarket on June 3, 2004." The topic for the "debate" between the prosecution and defense will focus on the key reasons for and evidence of this robbery.

A debate works the same way. Each debate has a topic. The topic is never the same; it changes from one debate to the next. The topic might be: "Middle school students should wear uniforms to school"; "Television is a bad influence"; or "The United States is winning the war on terror." The proposition team is responsible for making its case to prove the topic. They select their best reasons and evidence to present to a debate judge. The team does not have to prove its case beyond a reasonable doubt; it just has to show that the case is more likely to be true than false. The team tries to establish a reasonable proof for the topic.

Like the defense in a criminal trial, the opposition team in the debate will attempt to prove that the proposition team has not made its case. The opposition tries to find holes in the proposition's reasoning and evidence. It may also introduce its own arguments to prove that the proposition case is incorrect or even dangerous.

A debate judge will listen to the arguments and consider the reasoning and evidence from each team. She decides which team has won and also gives an individual score to reward the public speaking and argumentation skills of each debater.

The Middle School Public Debate Program rules for competition cover seven key areas of a debate:

1. Debate topics

2. Number of teams and debaters

3. Speaking order and speaking time limits

4. Preparation period

5. Debate materials

6. Points of information and heckling

7. Judge training and decision-making

DEBATE TOPICS

Topics for debate competition are usually announced two to four weeks before debates are held. MSPDP debating supports the use of both extemporaneous topics and impromptu topics. An *extemporaneous* debate topic is one that you can prepare before debating. You will have several weeks to think about the topic, research the main arguments for and against it, and carefully organize some notes about the better arguments. An *impromptu* topic is one that is not known before the debate is ready to begin. Students may debate extemporaneous and/or impromptu topics in the same competition. Topics are selected to provide a range of debate on personal, educational, social, political, economic, and cultural issues.

NUMBER OF TEAMS AND DEBATERS

Each MSPDP debate involves two teams: the proposition and the opposition. Each debate team is composed of three students. One student is the first speaker, one is the second speaker, and the third is the team's rebuttal speaker.

SPEAKING ORDER AND SPEAKING TIME LIMITS

Speakers make their presentations in the following order. The time listed is the maximum allowed for each speech.

First Speaker, Proposition Team	**5 minutes**
First Speaker, Opposition Team	**5 minutes**
Second Speaker, Proposition Team	**5 minutes**
Second Speaker, Opposition Team	**5 minutes**
Rebuttal Speaker, Opposition Team	**3 minutes**
Rebuttal Speaker, Proposition Team	**3 minutes**

The first four speeches (the five-minute speeches) are called constructive speeches. In these, each team will construct, or build, its arguments. Debaters may introduce new arguments in any of these speeches. The final two speeches for each side (the three-minute speeches) are called *rebuttal speeches*. These are summary speeches in which the debaters make the best case for their side and eliminate the major points of the other team. NO NEW ARGUMENTS ARE PERMITTED IN THE REBUTTAL SPEECHES.

PREPARATION PERIOD

A topic is announced before each debate. If it is an extemporaneous topic, debaters have twenty minutes preparation time to review their notes, speak with their coaches and teammates, and copy materials for use in the upcoming debate. If it is an impromptu topic, debaters have thirty minutes to prepare.

DEBATE MATERIALS

Before a tournament or competition, or during preparation time, students may review any information that would help them prepare for a debate. They may consult library books, current event articles in newspapers and magazines, Web sites and other information on the Internet, class notes, and written records of debate meetings and previous debates. They may speak to teachers, coaches, teammates, parents, friends, and others.

Once the debate begins, however, students MAY NOT REVIEW OR USE any materials, even handwritten notes, that were not prepared <u>during the preparation time period</u>. Most importantly, students may not read prepared speeches in a debate. Using pre-prepared materials is a serious violation of the rules, and may mean forfeiting or losing a debate.

POINTS OF INFORMATION AND HECKLING

Debaters use points of information and heckling, both parts of parliamentary procedure, during the debate. A *point of information* (also known as a POI, pronounced "P-O-I") is a request to the speaker to surrender some of his speaking time for a comment or question by the opposing team. The speaker may accept or reject a POI. If he accepts

only 1st debate ?
turnin research ?

a point, the POI must last no longer than fifteen seconds. The speaker accepts only a single point at a time. The person making a point of information must not interrupt the speaker's answer, make a two-part question, ask a follow-up question, or offer another comment unless the speaker agrees to it by accepting another POI.

A *heckle* is an interruption of a speaker during his presentation. The MSPDP style encourages responsible heckling. Students heckle to applaud teammates and opponents before and after their speeches. Heckling is done by slapping one's hand on the table three to four times. It is like applause, except the debaters use a table as the "second hand." Heckling is a sign of respect for your friends and opponents and is a way of showing support for all those participating in a challenging competition.

Debaters may also cheer the arguments of their teammates and show their displeasure with some of their opponents' opinions. They may slap the table in support of a particularly clever or winning argument and add a shout of "Hear! Hear!" to the pounding. During an opponent's speech, they may say "Shame!" if they strongly disagree with the speaker's opinion.

The MSPDP format includes points of information and heckling in order to encourage impromptu argumentation and public-speaking skill development. They make the debate exciting, interactive, and fun. Debaters can use these techniques long after their speaking time. It lets debaters stay involved both before and after their speeches.

Use points of information and heckling strategically to show the judge that your opponent cannot defend an argument or has made an error Never use them to distract a speaker or continually interrupt a presentation. Do not get carried away with POIs and heckling. A judge may deduct individual speaker points for rude behavior during the opposing teams' speeches. He may also reward individual speakers and teams for the effective use of POIs and heckling.

JUDGE TRAINING AND DECISION-MAKING

Each MSPDP judge must be certified. To be eligible for certification, a person must be at least a high school sophomore. Judges must decide the outcome of the debate carefully and fairly. Any judge who cannot do so should remove herself from judging. Judges are never assigned to debates involving students from their own school. The judge must determine which team argued successfully on the topic. If the proposition team proves its case, she will declare them the winner. If they did not, she will decide for the opposition. There are no ties; neither can two teams win or both teams lose a debate.

In addition to deciding the winning team, a judge must award individual points to each of the six debaters. Students are rated on a scale of zero to thirty points, with thirty points awarded for a perfect performance. The judge will consider public speaking, argumentation, and teamwork skills in assigning points. She may give the same points to more than one student.

After careful deliberation, the judge will complete a ballot, a record of the debate given to her by the tournament host on which the judge provides a detailed description of the reasons for the outcome and lists additional comments to help debaters improve their skills. She will then announce the outcome of the debate to the participating teams. She also will explain the reasons that a particular side has won the debate and provide some constructive criticism to help debaters improve in future debates.

CHAPTER 3

THE MIDDLE SCHOOL PUBLIC DEBATE PROGRAM FORMAT

THE MSPDP format requires a different topic in each debate. This format is particularly valuable for students because the more they pay attention to their subjects in school, as well as to the world around them, the more likely that they will be prepared for their debates.

UNDERSTANDING DEBATE TOPICS

The format helps students make connections among subjects. Although the topic may change, some arguments will appear from topic to topic. For example, several topics might require the proposition team to make a case for the U.S. government helping solve problems in other parts of the world:

- The United States should send peacekeeping troops to the Middle East.
- The United States should help solve African poverty.
- The United States should better protect global ocean resources.

For each of these topics, the proposition team would make a case that the United States ought to help solve a problem. But many people argue that the United States should not involve itself in the affairs of other countries. They maintain that the United Nations is better at solving international problems because it is more trusted and efficient. The opposition team could use a version of this argument for each of the three topics above. Students learn that the issue of agency—the individual, group, organization, or government responsible for acting on an issue—can be considered and debated on a variety of topics.

In addition, students consider other elements of public policy—economic factors (Is there enough money?), human resources (Are there enough specialists, like doctors or soldiers?), and social forces (Will people cooperate or resist a new law that tries to solve a problem?)—in examining a variety of topics. When you are faced with a new topic, look for the similarities between it and the topics with which you are familiar. You may already know some of the issues involved.

Using different topics makes debating fair. Debate on a single topic might favor some individuals or teams. For example, students whose parents are lawyers might have an advantage on a legal topic. Students whose parents are health care professionals or are in the health insurance business might have the upper hand on a health care topic. Some topics might give an edge to a student who is an immigrant, or has lived in different regions of the country, or understands poverty from personal experience, or has a large family. The benefit of debating in the MSPDP format is that no student has an advantage in every debate.

Debaters will know the majority of the topics before they attend a tournament. At a typical MSPDP tournament, each student will participate in five debates, each with its own topic. Students will know three or four of the five topics in advance, usually for two to four weeks before the event. One or two debates may be on an impromptu topic. The students may know the topic area, but they will not know the exact wording of the topic.

DEBATE TOPICS

The majority of the topics will be extemporaneous; students will know the subject in advance. Here are examples of topics that have been used in MSPDP tournament competitions:

- Cellular phones should be allowed in schools.
- The United States should significantly increase space exploration.
- Television is a bad influence.
- The United States should lower the voting age.
- Torture is justified for national security.
- Junk food should be banned in schools.
- State lotteries should be ended.
- School should be year-round.
- The United States should eliminate its own weapons of mass destruction.
- Peer pressure is more beneficial than harmful.
- Schools should not use standardized testing.
- Human cloning should be permitted in the United States.
- The United States should ban the death penalty.

There is a difference between a topic and a topic area. A topic is a focused statement that directs debate toward a narrow issue. A topic area is more general. It helps guide research and preparation for an impromptu debate but does not give concrete direction to a discussion. For example, in the topic area "U.S. elections," a tournament director could offer such topics as the value of the presidential debates, the benefits and costs of negative political advertising, raising or lowering the voting age, allowing foreign-born citizens to run for president, eliminating the Electoral College, or reelecting George W. Bush.

Here are some examples of topics and topic areas:

- Topic area: Energy policy
- Topic: The United States should reduce its use of oil.

- Topic area: School administration
- Topic: School attendance should be voluntary.

- Topic area: Human rights
- Topic: Torture is justified for national security.

To succeed in debate, you must think about the way the proposition and opposition teams will divide the arguments. On each topic, what would you expect the proposition team to say? What would you expect the opposition team to argue?

You must consider both sides of each topic for two reasons. First, you will know your opponent's arguments if you plan the same way she does. This is called *argument anticipation*. If you can predict what the other team will say, you can answer their arguments and outmaneuver them. Anticipation is a successful technique for sports, board games, videogames, and card games. In fact, anticipation is a skill necessary for all competitive events.

Second, although you often will know the debate topics prior to a debate competition, you will not know which side of the topic you will argue. At each debate competition, you will be assigned to the proposition and opposition equally. For example, at a tournament featuring four debates, you will make a case for the topic in two rounds and argue against the proposition in the other two. Because you do not know which side you will be assigned, you must prepare both sides of each topic.

But let's get back to the questions you might ask about a debate topic. Here are two topics used in middle school debate competitions;

- It is wrong to eat meat.
- Employees should be drug-tested at work.

What would you expect the proposition team to say on each topic? Which arguments would they select to prove the case? What would you expect the opposition team to argue? If you were on the opposition team, how would you answer the proposition's best arguments?

Often a topic's meaning is not as obvious as it seems, just like the meaning of a word. What does *cool* mean? Does it mean that the weather is a bit chilly? Or is it a description of someone with little emotion? Does it mean that everything is fine, or even very good? *Cool* means more than one thing. Topics do too.

Let's examine the topic "Schools should not use standardized testing." It may appear straightforward, but some of the words have more than one meaning. What, for example, is a school? We know that a school is an educational institution, but there are many kinds of schools. There are primary schools, middle schools or junior high schools, high schools, colleges, trade schools, journalism schools, law schools, film schools, schools of education, schools of nursing, and medical schools.

There also are many kinds of standardized tests. A standardized test is one that is the same for all students. In primary and secondary grades, students take standardized tests in subjects such as English, mathematics, and history. Students planning to attend college take the SAT or ACT tests. Many high school students take Advanced Placement tests for college credit. College students take standardized admissions tests for law school, medical school, and graduate school. Many school districts require an examination to graduate from the eighth grade and to earn a high school diploma. And these are just American examinations!

Is it reasonable that a proposition team would have to prove, in every single case, that schools should not use standardized testing? No! How could the first proposition speaker make a meaningful argument about every kind of school and standardized test? She would need more than five minutes (the time allotted for the speech) just to list the kinds of schools and varieties of tests. She could never begin her argument.

So what is reasonable? The proposition team defines the topic. Just as you would define what *cool* means so that people would understand your message, the first proposition speaker defines the topic, narrowing the discussion so that everyone can agree about the issue they will debate.

On the topic "Schools should not use standardized testing," the proposition team might argue that the debate will be about using the SAT or ACT in college admissions. Or they might argue that school districts should not require standardized tests for high school graduation. In these cases, the proposition team is announcing: "In this debate, schools will mean colleges, and standardized testing will mean the SAT or ACT," or "For the proposition's case, schools means high schools and standardized testing means a common test for graduation." In this way, the proposition team can focus the debate on a limited issue.

Some debate topics focus on personal or ethical decisions. Some are about school policy. Students may have a great deal of knowledge and strong opinions about some of these topics but may not have detailed knowledge of others. There are some other topics that will be entirely unfamiliar. Although you should research and review notes for all topics, you must carefully research new issues. Even when preparing well-known topics, remember that your opponents may have new material and clever ideas. You can always bring new thinking to a topic—that is one of the joys and challenges of debating.

To learn what kinds of topics are used in parliamentary debate competitions, look at the sample topics listed in Appendix 6. You may use them for practice debates or to test your skills.

UNDERSTANDING THE NUMBER OF TEAMS AND DEBATERS

The debate occurs between two teams: the proposition and the opposition. Each team has three speakers: a first speaker, a second speaker, and a rebuttal speaker. Each person delivers one speech.

The first four speeches are known as *constructive speeches*. Each is no longer than five minutes. The teams use these speeches to construct (build) their arguments. The teams will establish their strongest arguments and answer the major points from the other side in these speeches.

The *rebuttal speeches* follow the constructives. There are two rebuttal speeches, one for each team. In these speeches, each side summarizes their major arguments and explains why they should win the debate.

UNDERSTANDING SPEAKING ORDER AND TEAM RESPONSIBILITIES

You have already learned the speaking time and order for speakers. To review:

First Speaker, Proposition Team	**5 minutes**
First Speaker, Opposition Team	**5 minutes**
Second Speaker, Proposition Team	**5 minutes**
Second Speaker, Opposition Team	**5 minutes**
Rebuttal Speaker, Opposition Team	**3 minutes**
Rebuttal Speaker, Proposition Team	**3 minutes**

You probably have noticed that the proposition team begins and ends the debate. The first speaker for the proposition gives the first speech. The rebuttal speaker for the proposition has the last. This is another example of how the MSPDP format is similar to argument during a trial.

In a trial, the prosecution has the opening and closing arguments because it must prove the case against the defendant. If the prosecution does not make a valid or strong case, it will lose, even if the defense does not argue for its side! The prosecution side has the burden of proof. A burden of proof is a way of showing who is responsible for proving a case.

The proposition side has the burden of proof in a debate. They must show that their arguments are better than the opposition's. If they fail, the opposition team will win the debate. The proposition has the more difficult job. You may have heard the saying "It is easier to destroy than to build." The proposition has to build their case. The case must be logical and convincing. It must be strong enough to answer every major point from the opposition team. This is not easy.

The opposition team can succeed by showing just one major error in the proposition's case. If the proposition has left something out of their argument, or their argument is illogical, or they do not have evidence to support their reasoning, the opposition might win the debate. Because the opposition team's job is, in theory, an easier one, the proposition gets the advantage and responsibility of speaking first and last.

Despite the proposition's advantage in speaking first and last, the opposition team can dominate the middle of the debate. Look at the chart below. Because the opposition's rebuttal speaker follows its second speaker, the opposition has eight minutes of consecutive speaking time. In contrast, the proposition team has only the three-minute rebuttal speech to answer all major opposition points. As a result, the opposition is in a strategic position to overwhelm the proposition team.

Second Speaker, Opposition Team	**5 minutes**
Rebuttal Speaker, Opposition Team	**3 minutes**
Rebuttal Speaker, Proposition Team	**3 minutes**

SPEAKER RESPONSIBILITIES

Speaker	Time	Responsibilities
First proposition constructive	5 minutes	Makes the case for the topic, providing proof of the topic with three or four major points.
First opposition constructive	5 minutes	Makes several arguments against the proposition's case and refutes their major points.
Second proposition constructive	5 minutes	Extends and amplifies the original proposition points and refutes the opposition's major arguments.
Second opposition constructive	5 minutes	Amplifies the opposition arguments against the case and responds to the proposition's answers to the opposition's original arguments.
Opposition rebuttal	3 minutes	Explains why the opposition team should win the debate, finalizing the refutation of the proposition's major points.
Proposition rebuttal	3 minutes	Refutes the opposition's major points, summarizes the issues in the debate, and explains why the proposition team should win.

Each speaker has an important goal for his speech. The speakers also work together to make the best arguments and answer their opponents' major points.

First speaker, proposition

The first speaker for the proposition (sometimes called the *lead speaker for the proposition* or the *first prop*) opens the debate. Her job is to make the proposition team's case. She offers arguments to prove that the topic makes sense and that the case is more likely to be true than false. The speaker usually offers three or four main arguments, each supported by reasoning and evidence. The proposition team uses more than one major argument to give themselves several opportunities to win the debate. If they do not win on the first argument, they may convince the judge with their second point. If the opposition has a strong reply to the first three arguments, they may have a weak answer to the fourth point. The proposition team tries to increase the odds in its favor, hoping that they can win the debate on any of their major points.

Debate teams must make as many major arguments for their side as they can. In sports, a team can increase its chance of winning by scoring more points or runs than the opponent. The same is true in a debate. If the proposition team can score more points (make more major arguments) than the opponent, they are more likely to win.

You use the same strategy every day when you argue with others. Think about the way you convince your parents to let you stay at a friend's house overnight. Or the case you make to persuade someone that your opinion about clothes is better than theirs? How do you convince your friends to see a particular movie? You probably give several reasons to make one decision instead of another. This is making a case for your position.

Suppose you are assigned the following debate topic: "The United States was right to send troops to Iraq." A first proposition speaker might argue:

1. Saddam Hussein was a danger to his own people.

2. Iraq was trying to produce weapons of mass destruction (WMD).

3. There should be democracy in Iraq.

These are good points because they differ from each other. In a debate speech, you must do more than repeat one point three times. Your arguments must be independent. Each must stand on its own. If they do, each will be an argument that makes the case.

Once again, independent arguments in a debate are like the arguments used in a trial. A prosecuting lawyer needs to make her case. Suppose that the prosecutor is trying to prove that a defendant is guilty of burglarizing CDs from a neighbor's car. The prosecutor knows that two people saw the defendant break into the car and take the CDs. The police also found a pen, which belonged to the defendant and has the name of his business on it, in the car. The pen may have fallen out of his pocket during the burglary. Finally, the police found the CDs in the defendant's apartment. What should the prosecutor do with this evidence? Should she use only one of the eyewitnesses, confident that the testimony of a single person will be enough to convict the defendant? Of course not.

The prosecutor will use multiple, independent proofs to establish the defendant's guilt so that even if the defense has a reasonable explanation for some of the evidence, she will win her the case. Of course, the defense might be able to answer some of the prosecution's evidence. For example, the defense might prove that the victim borrowed the pen. If you were a juror, would you then find the defendant not guilty? Probably not.

If you were on the jury, you would listen to the other prosecution evidence. The victim would testify. You would hear that the CDs were stolen from her car. You would learn that there were two eyewitnesses to the crime. The eyewitnesses would testify that they saw the defendant break into the car and take the CDs. You would listen to the testimony of the police, who would report that the CDs were in the defendant's home. Even if the defense had an innocent explanation for the pen, you might decide that the prosecution has a strong case.

This is the advantage of multiple and independent arguments in a debate. If you present several ways of showing that your argument is true, you have more than one chance to win a debate. Now, let's go back to the example of the invasion of Iraq.

You need reasoning and evidence for each of the three independent points. Let's examine each of the arguments in order.

1. **Saddam Hussein was a danger to his own people.**

    Saddam Hussein was a tyrant who oppressed the Iraqi people. He protected a small group of loyal followers but persecuted the majority and kept them in poverty. He ordered the secret police to arrest, torture, and kill thousands of citizens who disagreed with him. He used chemical weapons against his own people, killing thousands of Kurds. Because he was a danger to tens of thousands of Iraqis, he had to be removed from power.

    The United States was the only country with the military strength and political willingness to use force to remove him. If the United States had not ousted Saddam Hussein, he would have killed and tortured many more innocent Iraqis. The United States was right in sending troops to Iraq because it eliminated Saddam's government.

2. Iraq was trying to produce weapons of mass destruction (WMD).

Although U.N. and U.S. weapons inspectors found no weapons of mass destruction in Iraq, they did find documents showing that Saddam Hussein wanted to acquire or build them. He tried to construct a nuclear weapon for many years, and he had made biological and chemical weapons. He used chemical weapons against his own people and against Iranian soldiers during the Iran-Iraq war.

Although he did not possess WMDs, he could have acquired them in the near future. Some nuclear powers, like Pakistan, have sold nuclear equipment and plans to other nations. Saddam could have bought them, and Iraq already had the scientists capable of making chemical and biological weapons.

The world should not wait until weapons of mass destruction kill tens of thousands of people. The United States was right to send troops to Iraq to eliminate the threat of WMDs.

3. There should be democracy in Iraq.

Democracy guarantees all people a voice in their government. Many Iraqis have never had this right. In fact, millions have never voted in a fair election because they were intimidated by the secret police and the military. The Iraqi people could not choose leaders who were concerned about their future. Millions have not received an education, health care, or adequate housing because of the corruption and oppression of the Saddam Hussein regime. The United States was right to send troops to Iraq to set up a new government that would give power to the people.

These major arguments could make the case for the proposition team. But is a list of arguments a speech? No! As you remember from Chapter 1, you cannot win a debate with just the best idea or an entertaining presentation. Persuasive public speakers deliver powerful arguments in a clear, confident style. They are both entertaining and informative. They cleverly use different kinds of public-speaking techniques, including organized and logical arguments, careful and proper use of words, simple and direct messages, powerful images, and interesting vocal delivery.

Your opening speech must be organized and persuasive. Follow the speech organization mentioned earlier in the book: introduction, main body, and conclusion.

Introduce yourself, state the topic for the judge and audience, and explain why it is important. Tell the judge what you will prove before you begin the main body of your speech. For example,

> Good afternoon. I am Jane Doe, the first speaker for the proposition team from Culver City Academy. I am here to discuss an important international issue. There are cruel people in the world who rise to power by threat, intimidation, and force. Sometimes they are a danger to their own people. On other occasions, they are a threat to the world community. Saddam Hussein was a person who was both a danger to the citizens of Iraq and to the people of the world. That is the reason I am here to make a case for the topic "The United States was right to invade Iraq." I will present three major arguments to prove the topic is more likely to be true than false. Any one of these points would win the debate for Culver City Academy.

This is an effective introduction that accomplishes all the speaker's goals. It:

- Introduces the speaker and the team to the judge and audience.

- Describes the importance of the speaker's message.

- Shows what is necessary to make the case (proves that the topic is more likely to be true than not).

- Shows the independence of the major arguments (tells the judge that only one major point is enough to win the debate).

Following the introduction, the first speaker for the proposition proceeds to the main body of her speech: making the case. In the case above, she presents the three main reasons why sending U.S. troops to Iraq was a good idea.

The speaker then concludes the speech, emphasizing that she has proved the case.

> Saddam Hussein was a tyrant. The United States was the only country that had the military strength and the willingness to remove him. Sending troops to Iraq helped the Iraqi people, protected the world

from the threat of weapons of mass destruction, and offered hope for democracy in the Middle East. The United States was right to send the troops to Iraq.

First speaker, opposition

The first speaker for the opposition team (the *leader of the opposition* or the *first opp*) begins her team's challenge to the proposition. In this way, the opposition team provides clash in the debate.

Clash means conflict or difference of opinion. Difference of opinion is one of the fundamental principles of any kind of debate. Clash is simply what happens when arguments oppose each other. The opposition team creates clash when it tries to prove that the proposition team has not made its case.

The first opposition speaker uses two kinds of tactics to argue against the case: direct and indirect argumentation. She may dispute the proposition's reasoning and facts. This is called *direct refutation*. She may point out inconsistencies or contradictions, show argumentative fallacies and errors in reasoning, give counter-examples, and explain how the proposition team has exaggerated the evidence.

To be effective, the first speaker for the opposition must address each of the proposition's major points. After all, the proposition knows how to make independent arguments, each of which could win the debate.

In the Iraq debate, the proposition presented three points. The opposition speaker, therefore, should organize her speech in the same way so that the judge can follow her reasoning easily. Of course, she will introduce her speech before answering the proposition case.

> There are cruel and dangerous leaders in the world, but this is not the issue for this debate. This debate is about solving the problems these leaders cause, and a U.S. military invasion is not the only, or best, solution to the problem.
>
> Good afternoon. My name is Kendra Smith, and I am from Clark Junior High School. On behalf of my teammates on the opposition, I am here to argue that the proposition's case is wrong in several major ways. In addition, the proposition team has not discussed some issues that will be helpful in deciding if the United States should have invaded Iraq. First, I will argue against the major points of their case and then make some new points for our side.
>
> As you recall, the main points of the proposition team's case are:
>
> 1. Saddam Hussein was a danger to his own people.
>
> 2. Iraq was trying to produce weapons of mass destruction.
>
> 3. There should be democracy in Iraq.

Let's examine the first point: Saddam Hussein was a danger to the Iraqi people. Yes, Saddam Hussein fought his own people and even used chemical weapons against them. But what country was his ally at the time, helping him to buy military equipment and giving him military intelligence during his war against Iran? The United States. It is inconsistent to say that the United States should overthrow him for actions he took with our help. The behavior of the United States leads other nations to see us as untrustworthy. It is why thousands of people who do not trust us are willing to become terrorists and fight us. Sending troops to Iraq shows other nations only that the United States might be the problem.

Now, what about their second point: Saddam Hussein was building weapons of mass destruction? If so, he did not do a very good job. No one has been able to find them. They aren't there. The proposition team is just repeating something that the entire world knows is false. Iraq did not have weapons of mass destruction. What do we know about WMDs? We know that U.N. inspectors found the weapons and destroyed them. We know that Iraqi scientists and the military were lying when they told Saddam Hussein that they were making them. That is why there are documents saying that Iraq was trying to build weapons of mass destruction. The facts do not support the proposition team's case.

About their last point: the United States is helping to build a democracy in Iraq. This just isn't true. First of all, you cannot build a healthy democracy with war, especially if the troops fighting the war are from another country and killing innocent people. We are an occupying power, and the Iraqis are angry and resentful. The Iraqi people will not follow the lead of a country that has made war on them. Would you? That is part of the reason that there is so much violence today in Iraq. Car bombings, attacks on the police, roadside bombings of U.S. troops, and serious crimes occur all over the country. Also, many Iraqis are worried that democracy might lead to civil war. If Iraq were to become a democracy, the Shiite Muslims, who comprise 60 percent of the population, would gain control. The Sunni Muslims, who were loyal to Saddam Hussein and are heavily armed, and the Kurds would lose power. The proposition's argument was that democracy gives a voice to the people. The Sunnis and the Kurds fear that democracy will take away their voice because they are minority populations. They might fight rather than lose their power to a Shiite government.

The facts simply do not support the proposition team's case.

The opposition could also clash with the proposition case through *indirect argumentation*. Indirect argumentation involves using relevant arguments that are not part of the proposition team's case. You use indirect argumentation all the time. Imagine that a friend has asked you to go to a movie. You agree but are not interested in the movie she wants to see. You might use direct refutation about her choice: "That's not a good movie. It isn't as funny as it is supposed to be. I know. I already saw it." You have made two direct arguments. First, you have said that the movie is not very good. It is supposed to be a comedy but it isn't funny. Second, you have already seen it. Seeing the same movie again would be boring. Because these issues discuss the movie your friend named, the arguments are direct. They speak to the issue she was discussing.

You may also add indirect argumentation to the conversation: "But I know a movie that is much better. James and Kathy saw it yesterday and really liked it." This is indirect argumentation. You are not directly discussing her movie choice. You are bringing new information to the conversation: a different movie. It is relevant to your discussion because you are talking about seeing a movie. You have another idea and have evidence to support it: your friends' good review of the other movie.

In the debate example, the first speaker for the opposition might use the following indirect argumentation.

> If the proposition team is correct and Saddam Hussein should have been removed from power, there was a better way to have done it. The United Nations or NATO could have sent troops to remove him. The coalition of nations that fought Saddam Hussein ten years ago, when George Bush's father was president, was more international and effective. It defeated Saddam's army and could have deposed him. The United Nations could have ousted him in 2003. Other countries did not want to go to war because they did not trust the U.S. assertion that Saddam Hussein was supporting terror and that he had weapons of mass destruction. And they were right. It would have made more sense to form a real international coalition to send troops to Iraq. This might mean more cooperation and less violence in Iraq today.

Of course, the first speaker for the opposition team will want a powerful conclusion.

> The proposition team has not made its case. They are still reporting information that everyone knows is false, for example, that Iraq was about to develop weapons of mass destruction. They are also trying to hide the involvement of the U.S. military in supporting Saddam Hussein. The opposition has presented the facts, and they disprove the proposition team's case. But more importantly, there was another way to eliminate Saddam Hussein. We could have used either the United Nations or NATO. This would have been better than sending in U.S. troops.

> The proposition team said that they had to prove that the topic was more likely to be true. It isn't. The proposition team's argument does not show that the topic is likely to be true. The opposition team from Clark Junior High has won this debate.

The finest first opposition speakers know that their best strategy is to use a combination of direct and indirect refutation. Direct refutation will eliminate your opponent's most significant arguments. Indirect argumentation will introduce new points that the proposition team will have to answer later.

The opposition does not have to disagree with every argument the proposition team makes. This strategy is ineffective and tiresome. Sometimes the proposition team might make a weak or trivial argument. Should you spend your valuable time discussing these? No, spend your time wisely. Point out that your opponents' arguments are weak, explain the reasons that the judge should ignore them, and move on to the important issues. Although you may be tempted to discuss your opponent's weakest arguments in great detail, doing so limits the time you have to answer their more powerful, perhaps winning arguments. Do not get distracted!

A better strategy would be to agree with some of your opponents' points—if they do not harm your position. Just because you are debating does not mean that you must disagree about every issue. Think about each argument and then decide whether to:

- Agree with it (and explain to the judge why the agreement helps, or does not hurt, your side).

- Ignore it (and explain to the judge the reason it should be ignored).

- Answer it.

Like the first prop speaker, the first opp speaker should not just make an argument but also make a speech. To do this, she should use all the techniques of effective public speaking, including a loud and clear delivery with appropriate emphasis on key words, effective eye contact and use of gestures, and a confident and poised manner. The first opposition speaker must answer the best arguments of the proposition team and present new arguments that will help the opposition. She must also tell the judge why each opposition argument is better than the other team's position. Why is the argument better reasoned? Why is it more believable? Why does it have superior, more recent, or more relevant evidence?

Remember that there are no ties in a debate. Always tell the judge that your ideas are better than your opponents' and explain why you win the debate. You must persuade the judge to vote for you and not your opponents. The more a debate appears tied, the better the chance that the judge will agree with your opponents' arguments.

Second speaker, proposition

The debate becomes even more focused after the first two speeches. The two teams have presented their opening positions. The judge and the audience know the best arguments for and against the proposition. Now the debaters must explore these issues in detail.

The second speaker for the proposition has three main responsibilities. First, she must answer all the objections of the first opposition speaker. If she can refute the points made in the opposition's opening speech, then the first proposition speech will stand. The proposition team will have made its case and will be winning the debate.

Second, the proposition speaker must point out any major proposition arguments that the opposition failed to address. Alerting the judge will help the proposition team to advance in the debate.

Third, the second prop speaker should add new arguments that might help her team's case. This speech is the last opportunity the proposition side has to introduce new arguments. As you know, the constructive speeches are the opening four speeches, the first and second speeches for each team. Debaters build their points in these speeches.

Either team may introduce new arguments during the constructive speeches. In the rebuttals, however, neither may do so. This is a very important rule. NO NEW ARGUMENTS ARE ALLOWED IN THE REBUTTAL SPEECHES. Consequently, the second prop speaker is the last speaker for the proposition side who may introduce a new idea.

It might be obvious to you that the debate would be unfair if debaters could introduce new arguments in the rebuttal speeches. For example, if the proposition team had the last speech in the debate, they could always save their best argument for the last speech and say, "Aha! The opposition has not answered the most important, the most powerful, and the most significant issue in the debate!" The proposition would then win every debate. In addition, the rule against new arguments helps the speakers focus their attention on the major points that might help the judge make a decision for their team.

The second speaker for the proposition must understand these rules. Her speech is the last chance for her team to present a new argument. If you need to say something new, DO IT NOW! You will not have another chance.

As mentioned earlier, the second prop speaker must answer the opposition's arguments. Imagine that you are the second proposition speaker in the debate that we have been following for the last few pages. How would you answer the opposition's arguments?

Here is the first argument your partner made:

> Saddam Hussein was a danger to his own people.

And here is your opponent's answer:

> Yes, Saddam Hussein fought his own people and even used chemical weapons against them. But what country was his ally at the time, helping him to buy military equipment and giving him military intelligence during his war against Iran? The United States. It is inconsistent to say that the United States should overthrow him for actions he took with our help. The behavior of the United States leads other nations to see us as untrustworthy. It is why thousands of people who do not trust us are willing to become terrorists and fight us. Sending troops to Iraq shows other nations only that the United States might be the problem.

The technique used in a debate to reply to the answer to an argument is called *argument extension*. An argument extension elaborates on an argument and answers challenges to it. To show the importance of argument extension, let's look at an example of an argument that does not have an extension.

The first proposition speaker begins with an argument we will call "X." The opposition answers the argument by saying the opposite. We will call this argument "-X."

Proposition	Opposition
X	-X

Now, let's think about this exchange as a mathematical problem. If we add the proposition and opposition arguments, what do we get?

$$X - X = ?$$

That's correct. The answer is "0." If the second speakers and the rebuttal speakers simply repeat the arguments of the first speakers, the arguments would add up to zero.

$$X - X + X - X, \text{ etc.} = 0$$

The judge must compare proposition and opposition arguments to determine who wins the debate, but if the proposition and opposition arguments equal a tie, how will the judge decide? Repeating earlier arguments is NOT a winning strategy. Instead, the second speakers for the proposition and opposition must EXTEND, rather than repeat, their partner's arguments.

To extend an argument, the second speaker for the proposition replies to the first opp's response to the original argument, making the proposition's argument stronger. How would this work with the first argument in the debate on United States troops in Iraq? Here is one example:

1st prop argument	1st opp argument	2nd prop argument
Saddam Hussein was a danger to his own people.	The United States helped Saddam Hussein attack his own people. The world does not trust the United States because we seem to say that Saddam Hussein is acceptable when he is on our side and dangerous only when he disagrees with us.	The United States may have helped Saddam Hussein in the past, but that was twenty years ago. Saddam has threatened, tortured, and killed thousands of his people since then. We have a new administration with a new attitude toward Iraq.

The second prop has answered the opposition speaker's opening argument. She has argued that the United States helped Saddam Hussein a long time ago. Circumstances have changed; the current administration has a different policy. Saddam Hussein had become a danger to the Iraqi people. Sending troops to Iraq protected the Iraqis. This argument supports the first proposition speaker's and eliminates the opposition's argument. It leaves the proposition team in a better position.

The second prop speaker must also point out any arguments from her team's first speech that the opposition ignored and answer any indirect opposition arguments. Finally, she should present new arguments to help make the proposition's case.

Remember to have a strong introduction and conclusion to your speech.

Second speaker, opposition

The second opposition speaker makes the final constructive speech for her team. The opposition can introduce no new arguments or issues after this speech.

The second opp has several options: extend the arguments from the first opposition speaker, answer the arguments from the second proposition speaker, or present new arguments. She should do all three. This speaker has the same opportunities and challenges as the second speaker for the proposition.

Like her proposition counterpart, the second opposition speaker needs to extend arguments. Let's look at how she could extend the first argument in our debate.

1st prop argument	1st opp argument	2nd prop argument
Saddam Hussein was a danger to his own people.	The United States helped Saddam Hussein attack his own people. The world does not trust the United States because we seem to say that Saddam Hussein is acceptable when he is on our side and dangerous only when he disagrees with us.	The United States may have helped Hussein in the past but that was twenty years ago. Saddam Hussein has threatened, tortured, and killed thousands of his people since then. We now have a new administration with a new attitude toward Iraq.

What should the second speaker for the opposition do?

1st prop argument	1st opp argument	2nd prop argument	2nd opp argument
Saddam Hussein was a danger to his own people.	The United States helped Saddam Hussein attack his own people. The world does not trust the United States because we seem to say that Saddam Hussein is acceptable when he is on our side and dangerous only when he disagrees with us.	The United States may have helped Hussein in the past but that was twenty years ago. Saddam Hussein has threatened, tortured, and killed thousands of his people since then. We now have a new administration with a new attitude toward Iraq.	It isn't a different government. The same people who helped Iraq in 1991 wanted to invade Iraq in 2003: Vice President Dick Cheney and Secretary of Defense Donald Rumsfeld. The proposition team is again wrong on the facts.

As the debate moves forward, each speaker should build on previous ideas. This is why debating is challenging. Each speaker must do more than the previous speaker. At the end of the debate, the team that best extends arguments will likely win.

Opposition rebuttal speaker

This speaker delivers the last speech for the opposition team. Her speech is the last opportunity this side has to explain why its arguments should win the debate. Rebuttals should be used to compare the major arguments of both teams. The opposition rebuttal speaker must prove that her team eliminated the proposition's strongest arguments and has made powerful and independent arguments of their own. She must select from among the many issues presented. With only three minutes, she cannot intelligently discuss twenty minutes of argument. She should include only the key and deciding arguments in her speech.

The opposition rebuttal speaker must play both offense and defense. The speech should have an offensive part, because the speaker must show why her side should win the debate. It should also have a defensive part, because she must show why the other side should not.

The opposition's rebuttalist must be careful not to merely repeat the issues her partners introduced. Simple repetition is not the best way to make a presentation—is not the best way to make a presentation—is not the best way to make a presentation.

The rebuttal speaker must use all the effective techniques of public speaking and argumentation, just as her partners have. She should have a well-organized speech, with an introduction, main body, and conclusion. If possible, she should follow the organization of the previous speeches. She should extend her teammates' arguments and answer those of her opponents.

Proposition rebuttal speaker

The proposition has the final speech in the debate. This speech should summarize the entire debate. The final rebuttalist should extend the proposition's most effective argument, refute the opposition team's arguments, and explain to the judge that the comparison of the proposition and opposition arguments means that the proposition side has won the debate.

This speaker should particularly beware of making entirely new arguments. Deciding whether an argument is new can be tricky. Saying "no new arguments in the rebuttal speeches" does not mean that speakers repeat their partners' arguments. The rule prevents the introduction of arguments that were never offered in the constructive speeches. If an argument was used in a constructive speech, the rebuttal speakers can discuss it and add new analysis and evidence to make it a better argument for their side. However, they cannot speak on an argument that has no basis in the constructive part of the debate.

This speaker has the same responsibilities and choices as the opposition rebuttal speaker.

TAKING NOTES IN A DEBATE

You cannot answer your opponents' arguments if you do not record and remember them. You must take careful notes during the opposing team's speeches to answer their points. In addition, you must take notes of your teammates' arguments so that you can extend them. What if your speech is finished? Do you still have to take notes? You will not be able to help your teammates answer your opponents' arguments during their speeches if you do not know what the opposing team has said. You will not be able to make effective POIs. You must take careful notes even after you have finished your speech. What if it is the last speech in the debate? You still should take notes. Your partners will want a record of their speeches so that later you can help them review their presentations. You will want notes of your opponents' best arguments and techniques because they might help you in future debates. In short, you should take notes of every speech in a debate. What is the best way to do this?

Participants and judges use a special method of note taking known as *flowing*. You must take good notes in this format to succeed in debate. For beginners, using a horizontal flowsheet with five columns is easiest. Most debaters will flow a debate on multiple pieces of paper to keep track of different arguments—but again, for beginners, start with one flowsheet. The flowsheet columns are labeled as in the diagram below:

1PC	1OC	2PC	2OC/OR	PR

Each column is labeled for a speech or speeches (more on that later): "1PC" is the first proposition constructive, "1OC" is the first opposition constructive, "2PC" is the second proposition constructive, "2OC" is the second opposition constructive, "OR" is the opposition rebuttal, and "PR" is the proposition rebuttal. "2OC" and "OR" are in the same column because the speeches are back to back and work together as a single stand on the floor for the opposition team.

Use each column to keep track of arguments made in that speech. Say that the proposition team makes a case for school uniforms. They might use three arguments:

- Cost. Many students cannot afford to look sharp every day, and students are embarrassed if they do not have the latest fashions.

- Distraction. Uniforms are not as distracting as the latest fashion and will help students focus on their class work, not their clothes.

- Violence. Uniforms reduce violence because students cannot wear gang clothes or symbols.

As the first proposition speaker makes her case, everyone else should take notes on their flowsheets. The first opposition speaker then refutes the case. She might introduce the issue of freedom of expression. She could say that requiring uniforms is a bad idea because students need to express their individuality in school. Then she would answer the arguments made in the proposition's case. On the cost point, she might say that uniforms are also expensive, particularly because people have to buy several at once. On the distraction point, she might argue that many things distract students and that districts have dress codes to deal with distracting clothing. Finally, on the violence point, she might assert that dress codes already prevent gang clothing and that uniforms will not reduce the gang problem because students join gangs even if a school requires uniforms.

The second proposition speaker answers the opposition's arguments while rebuilding and extending her team's case. The flowsheet will help her do this because she knows what arguments she has to answer and extend. She could answer the freedom-of-expression argument by saying that students have many ways to express themselves and that clothes are a shallow and unimportant method of expression. Then she can rebuild her team's case. To extend on the cost argument, she could reiterate it briefly before beginning her refutation.

> We said that many students are embarrassed because they cannot afford to keep up with the latest fashion trends. Now, they said that uniforms are expensive, but they are cheap compared to the latest pair of Nikes or Hilfigers. Wearing uniforms means that poorer students will not be made fun of for their clothes.

She would repeat this process for the other opposition arguments.

Speakers refute, extend, and compare arguments throughout the debate. Every speech, therefore, has a rebuttal component. Debaters present new arguments as well, but only in the constructive speeches.

1st Prop Constr.	1st Opp Const.	2nd Prop Constr.	2nd Opp/ Opp Rebuttal	Prop Rebuttal
There should be school uniforms.	Uniforms violate freedom of expression, limiting student choice.	Can express in other ways. And, clothes not that important.		
1. Cost. Many can't afford, and students are embarrassed if Ø have "right" clothes.	Uniforms expensive too—have to buy a lot at once.	Uniforms are cheaper than other options.		
2. Not as distracting; increases school focus.	Other things distract too. And, school dress codes stop this now.	Also, mean poor students won't be made fun of for clothes.		
3. Decreases violence: can't wear gang clothes.	Dress codes stop this too. Uniforms won't decrease gangs. Students join anyway.			

UNDERSTANDING THE PREPARATION PERIOD AND POINTS OF INFORMATION

At a MSPDP tournament, each round of debate begins with the tournament director or other person announcing the topic to the assembled students, coaches, judges, and guests. If the topic is an extemporaneous topic, the debaters have twenty minutes to prepare. If it is an impromptu topic, they have thirty minutes.

During the preparation time, debaters review notes, organize strategies with coaches and teammates, and think of new arguments. They write out any materials that they plan to use in the debate. Remember that you may not use pre-prepared materials during the debate, although you may use books, periodicals, notes, and advice during the preparation time. Debaters should think of possible points of information during prep time, too.

Teams may prepare in the classroom where they will debate or in another area. Traditionally, the proposition team uses the debate room for their preparation, if they wish. The opposition team then must find another location. Teams should not enter a debate room unless they will be debating there.

UNDERSTANDING POINTS OF INFORMATION

Points of Information (POIs) make parliamentary debating different from other forms of debate. As we noted earlier, a point of information is a request to the speaker making a speech to give some of her speech time to an opponent for an argument or question. Points of Information are made to the opposing team in a debate. You cannot make points to your own teammates. A debater may interrupt a speaker on the other team—provided she follows certain rules. She should not interrupt an opponent's speech unnecessarily, but some interruptions are acceptable.

In the MSPDP format, debaters can make points of information only during the constructive speeches (the first four speeches of the debate). POIs are not permitted in either rebuttal speech. In addition, they are not permitted during *protected time*, the first minute and the last minute of a speech. This gives each speaker an opportunity to introduce and conclude a speech without distraction or interruption.

The judge will signal that the opening minute of a constructive speech is over by slapping the palm of her hand once on her desktop. She will do the same with one minute left in each speech. The first sound informs the debaters that they may attempt POIs; the second tells them that protected time has begun. Debate rules permit points of information only between the two signals.

The time for a POI counts against the speaker's time. For example, if a speaker delivering a five-minute speech accepts a POI at the first opportunity (one minute into her speech), and the POI and her response take thirty seconds, she has three minutes and thirty seconds remaining in her speech.

Why would the speaker give up some of her valuable time? There are two reasons. First, a speaker wants to make her own POIs. If she does not allow POIs from the other team, they will not accept her POIs. Second, judges deduct points from a speaker who will not accept any POIs because it looks as if she is unsure of her argument or is hiding information from the other team. Because debaters want to show judges that they are capable and confident, they will make and allow POIs. On the other hand, if you accept too many points, you might appear to lose control of your speech. The best debaters will take many points without disrupting the flow of their speech.

To make a point of information, rise from your seat. You can also stand and say, "Point of Information," "Information," or "On that point." The speaker may take the POI by saying "I'll take the point," or simply, "Yes." Or she can refuse it

If the speaker accepts, make your point and sit down. Additional or follow-up statements or questions are not acceptable. After all, the speaker recognizes you only for a single, short point of information. If the speaker accepts a point, she should listen carefully and give a brief reply, then immediately return to her speech.

The speaker might also refuse to take your POI, with a brief comment (e.g., "No, thank you."). If the speaker does not take your point, you must sit down immediately. You do not have a right to interrupt the speaker.

STRATEGIC USES OF POINTS OF INFORMATION

Points of Information can be a powerful tool for debaters. They call the judge's attention to important issues and show your opponents' mistakes. They also can help you better understand confusing arguments from the other team. Points of Information have five main purposes: to understand an opponent's arguments, make clear the issues of the debate, evaluate evidence, advance arguments, and attack an opponent's arguments.

Seeking Understanding: You need to know what the other side is talking about in order to answer its arguments. You can make points to help you determine what the other team is arguing. For example:

- You said that you think it is a good idea for the United States to send peacekeeping troops to the Middle East. How many troops and to which countries will they go?

- You argued that television is a bad influence on children. Which TV programs are you describing? All television programs, including news programs?

Making Issues Clear: You do not have to challenge all your opponent's arguments. Sometimes, it is better to agree on some points so that you can focus your attention on the important issues about which you disagree.

For example, if the topic were lowering the voting age to sixteen, you might agree that getting more people to vote is a good idea. You might disagree that lowering the voting age is the best way to do that. For example:

> Point of information. (Speaker accepts the point.) "Can we agree that voting is a good idea and that more people should vote?"

The speaker might agree to this. As a result, you might not have to answer arguments about whether voting is a good idea. You can concentrate on the issue of having sixteen- and seventeen-year-olds vote. You agree on the importance of voting and disagree about the issue of age.

Evaluating Evidence: Debaters make mistakes about facts in debates:

- There are twelve members of the U.S. Supreme Court.
- The most underdeveloped European country is Hawaii.
- The United Nations was established in 1850, at the end of the First World War.

Points of information offer an opportunity to challenge facts and examples.

Advancing Your Own Arguments: You can use POIs to make arguments.

> Opponent: Point of information. (Speaker accepts the point.) "You claimed that increased prosecution of drug offenses will reduce drug use. That's not the case; it's never been true. Every time the government increases penalties, drug use and drug crime increase."

You can also use points of information to set up later arguments. For example, you can ask questions or make statements that deceive your opponent into thinking that you will make one kind of argument, when you intend to present a very different kind.

In the following example, we will assume that the proposition team presented a case arguing that the federal government should significantly expand its school breakfast and lunch program.

> Opponent: Point of information. (Speaker accepts the point.) "But the federal school breakfast and lunch program doesn't provide a well-balanced diet. It doesn't include dairy, does it?"
>
> Speaker: "Yes, it does include dairy. It provides all the necessary components of daily nutrition."

In this example, you have used a point of information that encouraged the speaker to make your major argument. The speaker thinks you will attack the school meal program because it does not include dairy foods. So the speaker tells you that there is plenty of dairy food in the diet. You then present your argument, which is that dairy food is bad for children.

- Dairy products increase childhood asthma, which affects tens of thousands of children each year
- Dairy products reduce immunity to bacterial infections. Because farmers add antibiotics to livestock feed, the medication is passed on to consumers. As a result, germs are likely to become resistant to antibiotics, leading to the development of very serious new infections in the future.

Undermining Your Opponent's Argument: You can use POIs to prove that your opponents' arguments do not make sense, are contradicted by other arguments, have no factual support, or are denied by better historical and current examples. For example:

- You have made the claim that nobody should be taxed without representation in government. Does this mean that child actors should be allowed to vote, since their incomes are taxed?
- You've argued there isn't enough money in the federal budget to pay for a new government program. But the government has a deficit and regularly borrows money to pay for programs. So wouldn't the government be borrowing to pay for your proposed program?
- You've argued that schools should have healthy snacks instead of junk food with a high fat content. But isn't it true that many of these healthy snacks have high sugar content and are also bad for you?

ATTITUDE DURING POINTS OF INFORMATION

Be polite during points of information because you are directly challenging a speaker. Even though you are speaking to the other team, your attention should be on the judge. Glance at your opponent when you begin to make or answer a point, but look at the judge while you make the point or give the answer. Looking at the other team during points of information may make you appear combative. Remember that you are trying to persuade the judge to vote for your side, not for the other team. Therefore, look at him.

ANSWERING POINTS OF INFORMATION

To be brief, be brief. Points of information should not distract from your message. Answer the point clearly but return quickly to your speech.

Avoid rejecting points by saying "Not at this time." (It only encourages your opponent to rise moments later. "Is this a good time?" Or moments after that. "Is this a good time?" "Not at this time." "How about now? Is this a good time?" "Not at this time.") Instead, say "No, thank you."

SUGGESTED EXERCISES

Practicing Points of Information

1. Read a daily news story with a teammate or small group of debaters. If you had to ask questions or disagree with the author, what would you say? Practice making some points of information. Can you challenge the information on the reasoning or the facts? Did the author leave out important information?

2. Have a debater present a three- or four-minute extemporaneous speech. Ask those listening to make a point of information. The speaker should be able to present his argument without being distracted, but he should accept a few POIs.

SECTION II
MAKING AND ANSWERING ARGUMENTS

Good public speaking techniques are not enough to win a debate. You must make sure that your speeches have solid, persuasive content. You might make great eye contact and have a loud and confident voice, but if you seem poorly informed or confused about your subject, you will not gain credibility with your audience.

This section teaches you some techniques for making and answering arguments using sound reasoning and good evidence. Good debating involves finding the best possible way to express an opinion. It requires the effective use of analysis, reasoning, and evidence.

CHAPTER 4:
MAKING ARGUMENTS

TO be an effective debater or public speaker, you must know how to make an argument. You may think that an argument is a verbal fight between people. This is one meaning of the word. However, in debates or speeches, arguments are defined as the *proofs* we offer to support our claims. One difference between everyday conversation and debating is that in debate you must back up your statements with good reasoning and evidence. Reasons and evidence prove your statements, encouraging your audience to agree with your side.

An argument begins with a statement: "Oranges are better than bananas" or "I deserve a good grade in this class." Note that these two statements are just that: statements. We call these statements *assertions*, because they claim something is true without providing reasons or evidence.

An assertion only begins an argument. The next step is to provide the reasoning. Think of this as the "because" part of an argument. When you offer reasoning, you are saying that your assertion is true *because*.

In debates, you must present the "because" part of every claim you make.

- Oranges are better than bananas because oranges are very nutritious.
- I deserve a good grade in this class because I have worked very hard this year.
- The death penalty is justified because people who kill others deserve to die.
- Schools should not be year-round because students will get bored and drop out.
- Television is a bad influence on children because it shows too much violence.

Reasoning acts to support each assertion by providing an explanation for why the audience should believe the claim. Of course, some reasons are better than others. Some make no sense at all, while others are confusing or seem irrelevant. Presenting reasons that are not strong or clear can weaken your claims. Consider how you respond to these assertions with their reasoning:

- The death penalty is justified because Victoria Smith says so.
- Schools should not be year-round because the economy is improving.
- I deserve a good grade in this class because the frost is on the pumpkin.

Not convinced? No surprise there. None of these statements includes reasoning that is clearly linked to the assertion. We do not know who Victoria Smith is, much less why we should care about what she says regarding the death penalty. The relationship between the improving economy and year-round school is not clear, and the less said about the frost being on the pumpkin the better. Any assertion has many possible reasons, but some are better than others. To convey your message, you must present the best possible reasoning for your claims.

Reasoning is only the second part of a complete argument. The third part, evidence, is just as important. Evidence completes your argument by supporting either its assertion or its reasoning, or both. You may have watched TV crime programs that discuss evidence: the bloody fingerprints that placed the accused at the crime scene, the taped phone calls that proved he planned to rob the bank, or the eyewitness that saw him running away from the scene. All of these might function as evidence in a trial, proving the assertion that the defendant is guilty. Evidence in debates serves a similar function. It backs up your statements and your reasoning.

AN ARGUMENT IS:

A: Assertion
R: Reasoning
E: Evidence

Even the best reasoning needs evidence for support. Life is full of occasions where things that make sense in the abstract do not occur in practice. For example, it is logical that people would abide by laws. Breaking the law carries penalties, and few people want to face arrest. Therefore, it might seem reasonable to solve a particular social problem by making it illegal. However, there is plenty of evidence that people do not follow all laws. Can you think of some laws that people regularly break? How about littering laws or laws establishing speed limits? To justify using a law to solve a particular problem, you would have to offer evidence that people would obey it.

To review, an argument is an assertion plus reasoning plus evidence. An easy way to remember this is to use the acronym ARE: Assertion, Reasoning, Evidence. To make a complete argument, you must include all three parts.

SUGGESTED EXERCISES

What's the Reason?

On a separate piece of paper, copy each assertion below and provide reasoning ("because…") for it. Remember that your reasoning should be strong and clearly linked to the assertion.

   a. Children should not have credit cards, because…

   b. All students should learn to play a musical instrument, because…

   c. People should not purchase sport utility vehicles, because…

   d. School should be year-round, because…

   e. When you are sick, you should go to the hospital, because…

   f. Internet music downloads should be legal, because…

   g. It is better to give than receive, because…

   h. The United States should reduce water pollution, because…

   i. Cellular phones should be allowed in schools, because…

   j. It is more important to study math than English, because…

What's the Assertion?

Below you will find several reasons. Your assignment is to think of an assertion that the reasoning might support. For example, for the statement "Because drinking soda is bad for the health of children," you might assert, "schools should not sell sodas to children." There is no one correct assertion for each reason. Pick the one you think is best.

a. Because our major streets are full of potholes,

b. Because video games are too violent,

c. Because drug use among teenagers is increasing,

d. Because the minimum wage is too low to support a family,

e. Because it is important to read books,

f. Because freedom of speech should be protected in schools,

g. Because the cost of a college education is too high,

h. Because eating breakfast is important for health and well-being,

i. Because many schools do not have computers for students,

j. Because it is important to protect privacy,

AN INTRODUCTION TO EVIDENCE

When you provide evidence for your arguments, you are communicating information that supports your conclusion. As you might expect, your ideas are stronger and more readily accepted if you back them up with solid evidence. We do not always offer evidence to support our claims in everyday life, but learning to use evidence and evaluate its strengths and weaknesses will serve you well in debate, school, and many other areas of your life.

Evidence comes in many forms. The most common type of evidence is the *example* or *illustration*. When you look at a dictionary, you may find that some words have pictures next to their definitions. These are illustrations, meant to clarify the meaning of the word by showing a concrete representation: an apple, a tree, or a chair. You offer an example when you describe a time and place when something has happened. Let's say you were arguing that schools should require students to wear uniforms. You might make the following argument, using an example:

> Schools should require students to wear uniforms. These requirements have made students happier. For example, when the city of Apple Crag required all students to wear uniforms, students reported that they felt more comfortable in school.

This is called an *historical example*, because it presents reasoning that was true in the past. The speaker uses the requirements in Apple Crag as an example to prove his point. All examples do not have to be historical. Some might deal with more recent events. These are called *contemporary examples.* You might also use examples from your personal experience to prove your arguments. Another word for an example is anecdote. An anecdote is a little story that illustrates your point.

Not all examples deal with current or historical events. Some are hypothetical, because they deal with events that have not yet occurred but might under certain circumstances. If you were arguing that schools should stop serving junk food, you might provide a hypothetical example to show the audience what the results of such a change might be:

> And so, if schools stopped serving junk food, students would eat more healthy foods like fruits and vegetables. For example, instead of eating a cheeseburger, they might eat a stir-fry.

Of course, hypothetical examples have not occurred, so they are weaker than historical and contemporary ones. However, using hypothetical examples can help your audience visualize your ideas.

To develop examples that prove your arguments, think: When has this been true in the past? What similar situations can I identify in my life or in the life of my community? How have those situations been resolved? Practice drawing connections between events so that you can use examples from one situation to reason about another.

Reasoning by example is a powerful way to prove a point. Proposition teams attempt to prove their case by showing how the current situation is harmful and how their plan would improve it.

Advertisers use similar tactics. A household products company may try to prove that the average toilet bowl is filthy by showing the Jones family's grimy toilet, thus creating a need for their toilet bowl cleaner. Then they might demonstrate that their product works by displaying the same toilet, cleaned to a blinding white. As a debater, you can use a variety of examples to prove your arguments. You might provide factual examples drawn from research or personal experience to strengthen your claim. You might also use hypothetical examples to draw the listener into your story.

Many people use faulty forms of reasoning by example, which an alert debater can use to his advantage. Thus you should carefully analyze your opponent's reasoning. Ask yourself:

- Are there enough examples to prove the claim?
- Are there examples that might directly counter the given examples?

BEWARE LOGICAL FALLACIES!

When reasoning from example, watch for logical fallacies. Two of the most common are:

- **Fallacy of composition.** This fallacy happens when the conclusion of an argument depends on the faulty transfer of a characteristic from the parts to the whole: "Jake likes fish. He also likes chocolate. Therefore, he would like chocolate-covered fish."

- **Fallacy of division.** The opposite of the fallacy of composition, the fallacy of division occurs when the conclusion of an argument depends on falsely extending a characteristic from the whole to its parts: "The average American family has 2.3 children. The Jones family is an average American family. Therefore, the Jones family has 2.3 children."

- Are the examples typical of the category for analysis?

Another type of reasoning is known as reasoning from analogy. When you argue from analogy, you are trying to show that what was true in one situation will be true in a similar one. An analogy is a comparison of people, places, things, events, or even abstract concepts. Debaters reason from analogy all the time. In making a case for nonviolent resistance to a political policy, you might argue that because such resistance worked in the American civil rights movement, it could work in another case as well. Advertisers also reason by analogy. In the case of the Jones's toilet, the advertiser clearly wants viewers to draw an analogy between the Jones's toilet and their own: "If the product worked on their toilet, it's bound to work in mine!" When analyzing analogical arguments, ask the following questions:

- How strong is the analogy? Are there differences between the two situations, people, events, etc. that the speaker is comparing? What are they?

- What are the similarities?

- Do the similarities outweigh the differences? Do the differences outweigh the similarities?

UNDERSTANDING STATISTICAL EVIDENCE

Statistical data is another common type of evidence. You encounter it when you read surveys or opinion polls. This type of data tells us something about a group of people or a set of actions or objects. You might see polls that say, for example, that 75% of people surveyed prefer flavored ice cream to unflavored ice cream.

Statistical evidence is commonly used to prove different kinds of arguments or establish different facts about the world. For example, if you could show that half of all American middle school students cannot find California on a map, you might use this to prove that our existing methods for teaching geography are failing. Or if you could demonstrate that 50% of the rivers in the United States are polluted, you might use this information to argue that we need to clean up our rivers.

Remember that statistics rarely represent all people. Instead, statisticians usually survey only a select number of individuals. When a poll says 80% of Americans support the president, for example, this does not mean that the survey-takers asked everyone's opinion. Instead, polls show that of the people surveyed, 80% supported the president.

The process of surveying a limited number of people is called *taking a sample.* One example of such a sample is the Nielsen ratings, which measure the popularity of TV programs. You may have seen articles about what kind of people (young, old, male, female, and so forth) watch and wondered how we know that. The answer is that the Nielsen Corporation installs boxes on the televisions of more than 5,000 households in the United States. These boxes record which members of the household watch which programs at what times. The company then collates this information to produce their ratings.

You might think that 5,000 households would not be enough to measure accurately what TV shows people watch. Accuracy, however, depends on which families Nielsen selected. A sample must be *representative*; it must resemble the larger population. Let's look at an example. If you make soup, you might include different kinds of vegetables: carrots, celery, onions, potatoes, green beans, and so on. Do you need to eat all the soup to find out what is in it? Of course not. You can have just one cup, and the odds are that it will contain the same proportion of ingredients as the rest of the soup. Of course, this does not mean that your sample cup is necessarily representative. You could have a cup that is all onions! Statisticians (that's the word for people who collect and do things with statistics) have to be careful to make their samples represent the larger picture.

When statisticians compile a representative sample of a larger item, they first find out what it is made of and in what proportions. One useful way to do this in the United States is by using the census. The U.S. Census is not just a head count; it also collects information on ethnic background, how much money citizens make, and what kinds of jobs or businesses they have. The Census uses some sampling as well as complete surveying to compile this data. (For more information about the 2000 U.S. Census, visit www.census.gov.)

Once statisticians know what the larger picture looks like, they can create a representative sample. For example, 25% of the people in Iowa are under the age of eighteen. If pollsters wanted to create a representative sample of Iowans, they would not select only people under eighteen, because most of the population (75%) is older. If they did, their survey would show only what young Iowans think, not what all Iowans think.

The selection of a sample for statistical evidence is critical. If the sample is too small, or if it is not representative of the larger picture, then the statistics themselves probably are not valid. However, most statistics you may encounter in newspapers, magazines, or on the Internet, do not include information about the sample size or the sample selection. You will probably just be given the data:

- 14% of students wish they had a monkey butler.

- 72% of parents enjoy dancing to disco music.

- 37% of people living in Weston, Connecticut, have red hair.

Are these "facts" true? You may never know because you do not have the information you need to evaluate these statistics. This does not mean, however, that you should accept statistical information only if it comes with a lengthy explanation attached. Rather, you must critically evaluate the sources: Do you trust the Census Bureau to give you accurate information about the United States population? How about CNN? How about Comedy Central? The source of information can tell you a lot about whether you can trust that information. You must ask, "Who did the study?"

You must also consider what the survey asked. People do not like to report negative information about themselves, even to anonymous telephone pollsters. If you ask how they are doing, most people will say they are okay, even if they are having problems at home or are worried about failing an upcoming test. Similarly, people in surveys report that they get more exercise, eat healthier foods, and watch less TV than they actually do. Is this because people are compulsive liars? No. Often people perceive their habits as different than they actually are. So what a survey asks matters in terms of the results. Simple opinion surveys are usually trustworthy, as are surveys that ask test-takers to choose from a menu of answers.

How a survey asks a question can change the answer. There is a big difference between asking someone the following questions:

- Do you cheat on tests?

- Are you still cheating on tests?

Question two is a loaded question, one that makes the respondent look bad no matter how she answers. If the respondent says "Yes" to question two, she admits that she is cheating on tests. If she says "No," she is saying that she used to cheats on tests. Either way, she loses. A similar kind of question is a leading question, one that suggests an answer. For example: "Isn't it true that you don't like math class?" This is different than asking: "Do you like math class?" Unfortunately, it is often difficult to find out what questions a survey asked and how they were asked—this usually requires looking at the original study.

One good check for any kind of evidence (statistical or otherwise) is to ask: Is there other proof to support this? The strongest evidence comes from many different sources. When this occurs, we say that there is a "consensus," that many sources agree about the issue.

Remember that statistics are not arguments. They are evidence that supports a topic. Let's look at an example. Perhaps you have come across a study that shows that the average American watches five hours of television per day. You would like to argue that this is too much. To prove this point, you cannot merely state the results of the study. You also will have to argue that five hours a day is too much. Too much compared to what? What else could people be doing with that time? What negative consequences might result from watching this amount of television? The evidence, by itself, does not prove that people watch too much television.

Give an Example

Below is a list of statements about various everyday events. Each statement ends with "For example." Complete each sentence with an example of the behavior, idea, or issue the speaker is discussing.

a. People today do not eat enough nutritious foods. For example,

b. Traffic in our community is really bad. For example,

c. Sometimes schools do not teach students the things they need to learn. For example,

d. All students should learn another language. This would help them in their lives. For example,

e. Many people are not interested in politics. For example,

f. Freedom of speech is important. For example,

g. People regularly break some laws. For example,

h. There are some things you cannot plan for. For example,

i. Sometimes, you need to be patient. For example,

Fill in the Blanks

In the chart below, each row represents a complete argument: assertion, reasoning, and evidence. Some arguments are missing one or more of their parts. Fill in the missing parts. Try to be specific.

	Assertion	Reasoning	Evidence
1	The minimum driving age should be raised to eighteen.	Raising the driving age will save lives by reducing accidents.	Sixteen-year-old drivers have three times as many crashes as drivers aged eighteen and nineteen.
2	Television is a bad influence.	Television shows too much violence.	
3	The United States should abolish the death penalty.		Since 1973, 108 people in 25 states have been released from death row because they were innocent.

4		Eating junk food is bad for your health.	Junk foods are high in fat and sugar. Too much fat and sugar puts you at risk for diabetes and heart disease.
5		Allowing younger people to vote would increase their involvement in politics and society.	
6			Evidence shows that students use their cellular phones to notify police and parents about violent incidents in school.
7	Schools should not use animal dissection in classes.		

THINKING CRITICALLY ABOUT ADVERTISEMENTS

Because you will make and critically evaluate arguments during a debate, you must understand what makes a strong—or weak—argument. The ARE formula for argument construction will help you. When a debater makes an argument, reasoning and evidence must support the assertion. Arguments with poor or incorrect reasoning and evidence are weak.

Learning to consider arguments carefully and thoughtfully can make you a good debater, student, and citizen. You can begin analyzing arguments by critically evaluating advertisements. You may not have considered this, but most advertisements are arguments. The assertion in the average advertisement is usually obvious: Buy this product! However the reasoning or evidence (if any) to support it may not be apparent, sometimes because advertisements play on ideas or assumptions that the audience already has. The advertisement may not explicitly (that is, out loud or in print) provide backing for its claim, but instead rely on the audience to fill in the blanks.

For example, you might see a toothpaste advertisement that shows a young person with unbelievably clean, white teeth, surrounded by a large group of adoring friends. Underneath the picture, the slogan might read, "BriteTeeth—Simply the Best." What are you to deduce from the ad? For starters, you might assume that the person attracted many friends because her teeth are lovely. The ad encourages you to conclude that her teeth are lovely because of BriteTeeth toothpaste. Therefore, you should buy BriteTeeth toothpaste. Let's look at the ad using the ARE formula:

Assertion: You need BriteTeeth toothpaste.

Reasoning: (Because) Using this toothpaste will win you friends.

Evidence: This girl has used the product, and she has lots of friends.

This advertisement offers reasoning and evidence, although it may not be good reasoning and evidence.

Remember that advertisements are trying to convince you to spend money on a product. One way to respond to these demands is to hand over your money. Another is to ask critical questions about the advertisement's claims. Consider this claim: "Twenty-five of the people we asked preferred new Mr. Sticky Syrup." What kinds of questions would you want answered before you purchased this product?

For starters, you might ask what these people preferred the syrup to: Did they prefer the syrup to bleach? You might also ask how many people were surveyed. What if the producers asked 10,000 people and only 25 of these preferred Mr. Sticky? Of the people asked, how many answered the question? How were these people chosen? Were they members of the Mr. Sticky Syrup fan club? Asking questions will help you identify weaknesses in the advertisement. In the case of Mr. Sticky Syrup, you can see that the advertiser has presented a weak argument. In other cases, it is not as clear.

SUGGESTED EXERCISES

Analyze the Ad

Below are four short claims made by imaginary advertisements. For each claim, develop at least three questions you want answered before you would buy the product. Write these questions on a separate piece of paper. Be specific!

a. Cats and their owners agree that no cat food is better than Fish-Ums!

b. You should try the great taste of Itsa Pudding, now with real milk!

c. I play a doctor on television. For a nutritious lunch, I eat a Flav-o-Bar!

d. Ninety-nine percent of teenagers surveyed say that Eagle shampoo is the best!

Find the ARE

Pick three different advertisements from magazines or newspapers. Determine what assertion each makes, what reasoning it offers, and what evidence it presents. Be specific. Present your results using the ARE chart below for each ad.

What product is being sold?_____

Assertion:_____

_____

_____

Reasoning:_____

_____

_____

Evidence:_____

_____

_____

Were you convinced to buy the product? If not, why? Was the ad's reasoning weak? How so? How could the reasoning be improved?

CAUSE AND EFFECT

One of the most common kinds of reasoning used in debate is causal. When you use *causal reasoning*, you try to understand what causes something. Thinking about causes and effects is not as simple as it may seem. You have already learned that the most basic kind of reasoning involves a "because" statement:

- I should get a hall pass because I need to go to the nurse's office.
- We should study math because we need to learn it to understand the world.

The word *because* can be used in several ways. You can use it to justify a belief, issue, or course of action (as in the examples above), or you can use it to show a cause and effect relationship between two things:

- You should buy this shampoo because it will make your hair shiny.

- I passed the class because I got an "A" on the final exam.

- The tree fell over because you chopped it down.

Thinking about cause and effect is also one of our most basic reasoning mechanisms. If you have ever spent time with a two-year-old child, you know that we are fascinated by causes at an early age. Young children constantly ask "Why?"

To find the cause of something ask, "Why did this happen?" To find the effects of something ask, "What happened because of this?" For example, if your car is out of gas, it won't start. Everything has a cause. Most things have many causes.

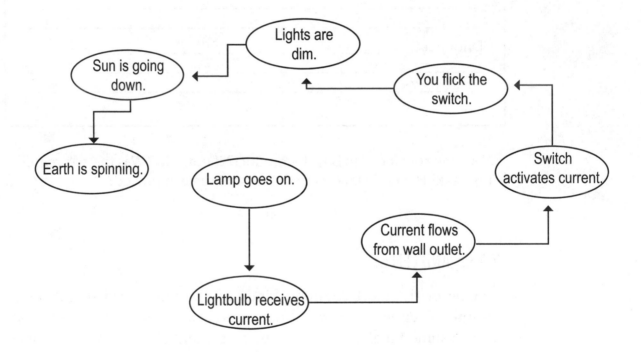

As you can tell from the example in the diagram, even a simple event such as a lamp going on has many causes, far more than we can show on the diagram above. For example, flicking the switch is not the only reason the current flows. It does so because your house is connected to a power grid, which is powered by a power plant, which works because it is supplied with fuel, which....

GUIDES FOR CAUSAL REASONING

1. **Nothing happens or exists without a cause.**
2. **A cause is not the same as a coincidence.**
3. **Determining a cause is often difficult.**
4. **Events can have both immediate and long-term effects.**
5. **Effects are often observed long after an event is over.**
6. **The effect of something often depends on the way we respond to it.**

Causes and effects can be quite complicated. Here are guidelines to help you use causal reasoning.

Nothing happens or exists without a cause. This is common sense. Just because you may have difficulty determining a cause does not mean one does not exist.

A cause is not a coincidence. If one thing comes after another thing, can we say that the first caused the second? Not necessarily. Let's say that you get up at 6 AM. The sun comes up at 6:01. Your awakening did not cause the sun to rise, even though one event came before the other. Here's another example. You're in a video store looking for a particular movie, but cannot find it. Just as you leave, another person returns the movie you want. Did your leaving cause this person to return the movie? Or was this simply a coincidence? A coincidence is when two things happen at the same time with no apparent connection.

Determining a cause is often difficult. You may have studied the rise and fall of the Roman Empire in your history classes. Many factors—military, social, economic, and political—contributed to its collapse. The diagram below lays out some of the causes:

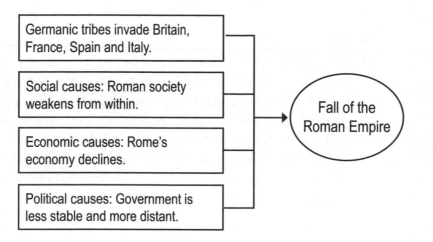

It is difficult to say which causes were most important. Certainly the invasions of Germanic tribes were the immediate cause of the empire's fall, but other causes contributed to its collapse. In order to prove that one cause is more significant than another, you have to make an argument.

Events can have both immediate and long-term effects. If your car runs out of gas, the immediate result is that it will not start. The long-term results may be more complicated. For example, you might miss work. This might cause you to lose your job, which means that you cannot buy the concert tickets you wanted. Some events cause a chain reaction: One thing leads to another, leading to another, and so on.

Effects are often observed long after the event is over. Let's say your car runs out of gas. You can expect that your car will not start. You also might foresee that you will miss work. However, you might not anticipate losing your job and not being able to buy concert tickets. Sometimes we cannot predict the specific consequences of an action until long after it is over. This is where a good knowledge of history (or a good memory) can help. Looking at similar issues in the past can help you to estimate what the results of an action might be.

The effect of something often depends on the way we respond to it. The effects of an action are not predetermined. The way we respond to an event can dramatically change its results. For example, consider what might happen if you started a fire while you were cooking. When you noticed the fire, you might run screaming from the house. Or you might use your fire extinguisher. Or you might call the fire department. Each response would change the results of the fire.

SUGGESTED EXERCISES

Explain the Effects

Below is a list of events. Pick one and brainstorm three results. Give a one- to two-minute speech in which you present the event and its potential results. For example, if your topic were "Earthquake," you might expect that an earthquake would destroy buildings, panic the public, and cause numerous deaths. In your speech, you should elaborate on each of these effects, helping the audience to visualize what might happen. Include an introduction and conclusion to make your speech complete.

  a. A major flood

b. Winning the lottery

c. A large forest fire

d. Getting accepted to a major university

e. Joining the army

f. Cleaning your house

g. Breaking an arm

h. Walking your dog

Explain the Causes

Brainstorm at least three things that could have caused each event listed below. Remember that events have more than one cause, and some causes may be more important than others. Be specific.

a. You decide to go to college.

b. You eat a salad for dinner.

c. Roger turns off his television.

d. There is an election at your school.

e. All schools stop selling junk food.

f. The United States allows people to have handguns.

g. Students bring cellular phones to school.

h. You break your arm.

COSTS AND BENEFITS

In many debates, you must evaluate whether an action does more harm than good. One way to determine this is to examine its possible effects. What would the action cause? What would it prevent? Do the benefits outweigh the costs? Only then can you decide if you should take an action or not.

You use this type of reasoning every day. For example, you check for traffic before crossing the street so that you avoid being hit by a passing car. You do not (we hope) experiment with being hit by a car just to see if the effect is harmful. Instead, you consider an accident a potential effect of a particular kind of behavior (reckless street-crossing). You evaluate the costs and benefits of crossing the street. The costs are the bad effects, while the benefits are the good ones. All actions have multiple costs and multiple benefits:

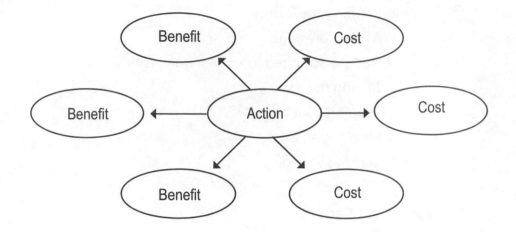

In debates, you must explain the costs and benefits of actions. Depending on what side of an issue you are arguing, you will often have to contend either that the costs of a decision outweigh its benefits or the benefits outweigh its costs.

Suppose that you must decide whether the school board should build a new school. First, you must consider the benefits of doing so. Is there a need for a new school? If so, why? Perhaps the existing schools are so overcrowded that students cannot learn. Maybe building a new school would mean that students who lived in that neighborhood would not have to ride buses across town. You must also consider the potential costs of building a new school. Perhaps building the new school would mean that there would be no money for textbooks in existing schools. Maybe it would be better to add on to current schools than it would be to build a new school.

Good decision-making is not just about counting the number of costs versus the number of benefits. You must consider whether the combined benefits would outweigh the combined costs, or vice versa.

SUGGESTED EXERCISES

Costs and Benefits

In the chart below, you will find columns labeled *action*, *benefits*, and *costs*. Pretend that you are considering whether to take each action. Provide at least two costs and two benefits for each. Do the benefits outweigh the costs? Why or why not? Explain. What decision would you make for each proposed action?

Action	Benefits	Costs
The city council is considering spending two million dollars to improve roads. Is this a good idea?	1. 2.	1. 2.
Should the school board hire fifty new teachers for middle schools in the district?	1. 2.	1. 2.
Should you quit the baseball team to work on the school newspaper?	1. 2.	1. 2.
Your state is considering a ban on sport utility vehicles. Would this be a good or a bad idea?	1. 2.	1. 2.

CHAPTER 5:
ANSWERING ARGUMENTS

YOU cannot win debates simply by making arguments or points for your side. Debates involve the exchange and comparison of ideas. You must argue against your opponents' points and show why your arguments are more important or more likely to be true. In this chapter, you will learn how to answer your opponent's arguments. An argument begins with a statement: "Oranges are better than bananas" or "I deserve a good grade in this class." Note that these two statements are just that: statements. We call these statements assertions, because they claim something is true without providing reasons or evidence.

BASIC REFUTATION

When you respond to an argument the other side makes in a debate, you refute that argument. The act of responding to an argument is called *refutation*. To improve your debate skills, you must practice refuting arguments of different kinds. In a debate, both sides will make many arguments. To show that you are winning, you must "play defense" against your opponent's arguments while "playing offense" with your own. A debate cannot be merely an exchange of unrelated ideas.

> **Speaker 1:** Bananas are better than apples because they contain more potassium.
>
> **Speaker 2:** Circles are better than squares because their shape is more pleasing to the eye.

This discussion is missing what in debate we call *clash*. Both speakers are advancing arguments, but their statements are unrelated. Clash is one of the fundamental principles of any debate. Unless arguments clash, there is no way to compare them.

You can answer an argument in many ways. Of course, some methods are better than others. The first way of refuting a claim is to provide a counterclaim, for example:

> **Speaker 1:** Bananas are better than oranges because they contain more potassium.
>
> **Speaker 2:** Speaker 1 says that bananas are better than oranges, but I disagree. Oranges are better than bananas.

Speaker 2 has merely provided a claim to counter the assertion of the first speaker. Who wins this debate? Clearly, Speaker 1 has the edge because she is the only debater who provided reasoning for her claim ("because they contain more potassium"). Good reasoning always trumps no reasoning.

A more advanced method of refutation provides reasoning for a counter-assertion:

> **Speaker 1:** Bananas are better than oranges because they contain more potassium.
>
> **Speaker 2:** Speaker 1 says that bananas are better than oranges, but I disagree. Oranges are better than bananas because they contain more vitamin C.

What makes this refutation better than Speaker 2's previous attempt? Here, she provides reasoning for her claim ("because they contain more vitamin C"). If you were judging this debate, how would you decide who wins? You find that Speaker 1 has proved that bananas contain more potassium than oranges. You also find that Speaker 2 has established that oranges contain more vitamin C than bananas. Neither debater has the edge. While there is direct clash between the assertion and the counter-assertion, there is no direct clash between the reasoning for each claim. Speaker 2 has not completely refuted her opponent's argument.

Complete refutation is important to win decisively when arguments clash. In order to refute an argument, you must include a "therefore" component that explains why your argument trumps your opponent's. For example:

> **Speaker 1:** Bananas are better than oranges because they contain more potassium.
>
> **Speaker 2:** Speaker 1 says that bananas are better than oranges, but I disagree. Oranges are better than bananas because they contain more vitamin C. Therefore, you should prefer oranges because, while many foods contain potassium, few contain much vitamin C. It is more important to eat oranges whenever possible than it is to eat bananas.

Speaker 2 wins. She has completed the process of refutation by including a "therefore" component. Note how the last part of her argument works. She compares her reasoning to Speaker 1's to show why her argument is better.

FOUR-STEP METHOD

1: "They say...."

2: "But..."

3: "Because..."

4: "Therefore..."

Almost all refutation can follow a basic four-step method:

Step 1: "They say...." Refer to the argument you are about to refute so that the judge can follow your line of thought easily. Unlike the bananas/oranges example above, debates contain many arguments. Unless you directly reference the argument you are discussing, you risk confusing your listeners. Confusion is not a good technique for winning debates. Good note-taking skills will help you track arguments.

Refer to your opponent's argument quickly. Rephrase the argument you are about to refute in a few words to maximize your speech time: "They say that welfare helps the economy, but..."; or "They say Batman is better than Superman, but... ."

Step 2: "But I disagree...." State your counter-argument. This can simply be the opposite of your opponent's claim. It can also be an attack on your opponents' reasoning or evidence. State your point clearly so that your judge, audience, and opponents can easily remember it.

Step 3: "Because ...." Offer reasoning to enforce your counter-argument. Your reasoning can be independent support for your counter-claim, as in the case above (Oranges are better than bananas because...). You can also offer reasoned criticism of the opposition's argument.

Step 4: "Therefore...." Conclude by comparing your refutation to your opponents' argument and showing why your point defeats theirs. You can do this by evaluating their evidence, the relative strength of their reasons, or both. You must develop a variety of strategies for argument comparison and evaluation to be a successful debater.

You must show that your argument is better than your opponents' because:

- It is better reasoned. Perhaps their argument makes an error in logic or reasoning.

- It is better evidenced. Maybe your argument makes use of more evidence. Perhaps your sources are better qualified than theirs, or your evidence is more recent than theirs.

- It is empirical. When we say that an argument is empirically proven, we mean that it is demonstrated by past examples. Perhaps your argument is proven by past experience, while theirs is not.

- It takes theirs into account. Sometimes your argument may take theirs into account and go a step further: "Even if they're right about the recreational benefits of crossbows, they're still too dangerous for elementary school physical education classes."

- It is more significant. You can state that your argument has more significance than theirs because it matters more in any given individual circumstance or applies to a larger number of cases. For example, if an issue is a serious one, such as a life-or-death matter, your argument is of great significance, even in a single case. If an issue is less important than immediate life-or-death, such as a common cold, but your argument applies to a great number of people, it might also be significant. The best arguments matter a great deal in an individual case and apply to a large number of cases (environmental crises, humanitarian emergencies, wars and civil conflict, unemployment, business bankruptcies, etc.).

SUGGESTED EXERCISES

Play a Game of "I disagree"

1. Ask everyone in your class to write down an assertion. Put them into a hat and pass the hat around. Have each student take an assertion and refute it aloud or on paper using the four-step method. Repeat this exercise with a partner. Have one person make an assertion while the other refutes it. Switch roles after ten assertions.

2. Using the four-step method, refute each of the following claims:

- Violent video games should be banned.

- All children under eighteen should have an 8 PM curfew.

- There should be a draft for military service.

- Parents should not buy war toys for their children.

- Schools should ban animal dissection in class.
- Television is a bad influence.
- The government should increase taxes.
- Students should wear uniforms.
- Schools should not require math classes.
- Violence is never justified.

CHAPTER 6:
LEARNING TO RESEARCH

ONE of the most important skills you need for effective debating is the ability to conduct good research. You may be the world's greatest speaker, but without good information organized and presented in a logical way you will not convince many people that your points are correct. You must learn how to do effective research.

Start your research by talking to teachers, especially those who teach in the area of your topic. Also talk to your family or people in your community about their ideas or opinions on the issue. This process will give you an idea of the types of arguments you might hear on both sides of the debate, but it is only the first step in your research. At some point, you will have to consult other sources. Learning how to research will broaden your perspective and help you in debates and in school.

STARTING WITH BLANK PAPER: SETTING A RESEARCH AGENDA

Most students do not know how to research for a successful debate. They find an article or two on their topic and declare their task completed. But the process of analyzing and researching an issue is more complex than just typing keywords into a search engine or a library database.

KEY RESEARCH QUESTIONS

Ask yourself the following questions:
- What do I know about this issue?
- What don't I know about it?
- Who does this issue affect?
- How does the issue affect them?
- Why is this issue important?

Use an Issue Analysis Form (see Appendix 1) or a blank piece of paper to help you plan your research. First ask: **What do I know about this issue?** List everything that comes to mind. You may think you know nothing, but this is seldom the case. Even if you are not familiar with the specific issue, you may know something about related ones.

Suppose you are researching the topic "International trade helps the poor." You might know nothing about international trade or what it has do with people being poor. However, you might know what trade is: the exchange of things or services. From this commonsense understanding of trade, you might guess what international trade is. You might also know what it means to be poor and some ways in which the poor are helped or hurt. Finally, you might guess that there are many poor people in the world. Before you move on to the next step, just stop and think about the issue. Given what you have guessed about international trade, and what you know about helping or hurting the poor, what are your initial reactions to the topic? Do you think it is more likely to be true than false? Why or why not?

Now ask yourself: **What don't I know about this issue?** Write down questions you have about the issue. On this topic, you might ask: "What is international trade?" or "What does international trade have to do with poverty?" You might also ask: "What are some ways that international trade affects the poor?" Ask as many questions as you like. The first steps in issue analysis help you set a research agenda, a plan for your upcoming research. Your questions will direct your research.

One important part of issue analysis is determining why the issue matters and to whom. To research an issue effectively, you must learn who it affects and who currently makes decisions about it. Answering these questions will help you determine why (or if) the issue is important, and what potential costs and benefits are involved. Ask yourself: **Who is affected by this issue? How?** From the wording of the topic we are discussing, you might guess that the poor and people engaged in international trade (such as companies or governments) are affected.

Finally, ask: **Why is this issue important?** You might have no idea, but you should develop some thoughts. The language of our topic suggests that trade influences poverty, so you should think about why helping the poor is important and write down your ideas. Think of as many reasons as you can. Do not worry about whether you are correct. At this point it is okay to speculate.

When you begin researching an issue, you need to get background information on the subject, even if you think you know a lot about it.

Reading a general article or two on the issue will help you gain perspective and find out how other people think about it. You can then anticipate what others might say in a debate on the subject.

SUGGESTED EXERCISES

Practice Issue Analysis

Complete an Issue Analysis Form (see Appendix 1) for each of the following topics. Compare your form with those of your classmates. Did you ask similar questions? Did the other students have ideas that answer some of your questions? Work with two other students to research the topic and find answers to your questions. Then present your answers to the entire class.

1. Television is a bad influence.

2. All middle schools should require students to wear uniforms.

3. The United States should lower the voting age.

4. The Internet does more harm than good.

BEGINNING YOUR RESEARCH: TELEVISION NEWS

Make yourself aware of the world around you. Identify current issues that face your school, your community, your nation, and the world. Watch one TV news broadcast every day. If you are watching a local news broadcast, the focus will be primarily on local events—city council meetings, crime reports, weather, and sports. For information about national and international news issues, watch a national news broadcast on a major network.

When watching the news, list the major issues covered, and follow them as they develop. Find answers to such questions as:

- What's the event?
- Where is it happening?
- Who is affected?
- How many people are affected?
- What is happening to those people, and why do they care?
- Why is the event happening?

- What solutions are being proposed?
- Who is proposing them?
- What effects will the solutions have?

Most news stories deal with controversial topics—that's part of what makes them news. Normally, a story will include comments from people on many sides of an issue. These quotes are called *sound bites*, because they are usually small parts (bites) of a larger statement the person made. You must evaluate sound bites critically because you may not know the context in which the comments were made.

As you explore the information available on television, move beyond commercial network news. Public television has many good news programs that offer in-depth coverage of issues. One of the best is the documentary series *Frontline*, shown on PBS every week. Commercial network programs such as *Dateline* and *60 Minutes* provide excellent, well-researched information on current events as well. Cable television also has several major news shows.

Other types of TV programs are also good sources of information. For example, the *National Geographic Explorer* reports on events from all over the world. The History Channel has many valuable programs that compare the past to the present or analyze historical events. These programs can be important for debate research because they give you a wide base of information from which to draw examples. Remember that one purpose of research is to enable you to generate examples on different issues.

Keep your research notes in a composition book or another small notebook that will help you track and organize your information gathering.

GETTING IT IN PRINT: READING THE NEWSPAPER

A second step you can take to improve your research skills is to read the newspaper. Reading a newspaper is different from watching the TV news in several ways. We are usually passive when we watch television. We let its programs wash over us. However, the act of reading requires more concentration. Also, we can be easily distracted while we read. In contrast, it is harder to become distracted while watching television, as its colors and flickering lights can create a hypnotic effect on the viewer.

Newspapers cover more stories than the television news because they have more space and are not confined to a specific time slot (minus commercials!). Sometimes it is hard to read an entire newspaper because many of the stories do not seem interesting or relevant. At least when you see a story on the TV news, it is over within a minute or two.

All newspapers are not alike, and some are better than others. Generally, small local papers are good at covering local or state issues but do not include original reporting on national or international stories. They often rely on news wires or news services for their national or international stories. A news wire is a service that provides reports and pictures to hundreds or thousands of newspapers for a fee. Newspapers will print these reports with a byline that includes the name of the news wire. AP (Associated Press), Scripps-Howard, and Knight Ridder are some of the major U.S. news services. There is nothing wrong with wire stories. They usually are written by experienced reporters who are employed by the service rather than by a paper.

Large newspapers have their own reporters to cover national and international stories and so rely less on news services. These papers are usually located in major cities and are read throughout the country. Major newspapers work very hard to develop a reputation for good reporting and solid coverage of major events. Some of the best U.S. newspapers include:

- *The Boston Globe*
- *The Christian Science Monitor*
- *The Los Angeles Times*
- *The New York Times*
- *The Philadelphia Inquirer*
- *The Wall Street Journal*
- *The Washington Post*

Do not despair if your local newsstands do not carry these papers. If you want to use them, you can always read them on the Internet. Most are free online.

Most newspapers are divided into several sections. The front section contains the major national, international, and local stories. Other sections may cover sports, hobbies, or business. Normally you will find the information most relevant for debating in the front section. When you pick up a newspaper, note how the stories are presented. There may be a fold in the front section. The stories above the fold are designed to catch the eye, to interest the reader, and to present the most important issues of the day. Newspapers use headlines to summarize and encourage you to read the story. Headlines are in larger type than the stories and may also have a smaller headline below them:

Schools Eliminated Forever

Students Have "Learned it All," Teachers Claim

Anytown, USA—January 5

ROGER REPORTER, *IDEA News Service*

A dateline under the headline tells you from where the story was sent and on what date. Often a byline follows the dateline. It identifies the reporter and her affiliation. In the example above, the story is by Roger Reporter, who works for IDEA News Service. If the byline does not include an affiliation, a staff writer, a reporter employed by the newspaper, wrote the story..

Newspaper stories begin with a lead, which is similar to a speech introduction. It is a sentence or a paragraph that tries to involve the reader in the story while introducing the themes to come. Most newspaper stories pack the key information into the first paragraph. This information usually includes the answers to the essential questions in journalism:

- WHO?
- WHAT?
- WHEN?
- WHERE?
- WHY?
- HOW?

The body of the story follows the lead. It has a structure resembling an upside-down pyramid. The most important information comes early in the article, and other information—additional examples, further interviews, or more details—follows.

Newspapers contain different kinds of stories. Some report events. Others, called investigative reports, present in-depth inquiries into events or issues. Editorials express an opinion about the news. Most newspapers have at least one page of editorials. Some editorials have a clearly marked author, others do not. Editorials without an author represent the opinions of the paper's editors. The editorial pages are valuable resources for debaters because they critically evaluate the issues of the day. They are similar to debate speeches, in which you have to take a side on an issue and argue your points. Examine the editorials closely to see what kinds of arguments they make and what kinds of evidence they offer to support them.

How should you read the newspaper? Although you do not have to read the entire paper every day, avoid reading only those stories that interest you. Study at least one story on an unfamiliar issue to help you broaden your knowledge. Newspapers cover many of the stories you see on the television news. Make sure you read the articles about these so that you can compare the information presented. Do the stories differ, or are they similar? How is the coverage of the issue different? Did the newspaper interview different people? Do those people seem more credible, or less? How so? Remember to keep notes from your daily research in your notebook.

MORE IN-DEPTH? MAGAZINES AND JOURNALS

Magazines and journals are important for researching debate issues. These publications are also called *periodicals* because they come out at regular intervals—every week or month, for example. Thousands of periodicals are published in the United States every year. Many of these contain thoughtful, well-researched reporting and analysis—just the thing for aspiring debaters. You may be familiar with the three most popular U.S. news periodicals: *Time, Newsweek*, and *U.S. News & World Report*. These widely available magazines appear weekly. Although they contain much useful information, particularly for the beginning researcher, they are not the only periodicals you should investigate. A good way to become familiar with a variety of magazines and journals is to go to your local library and browse the shelves of current periodicals. Pick up different magazines and leaf through them. What subjects do they deal with? Do they seem to be specialized or general? Do they contain interesting facts or stories? Do the authors of articles seem qualified?

Magazines and journals approach stories differently than newspapers. Although both may have information about the same issues, magazines sometimes cover these issues in more detail because they are not under the pressure of publishing daily. Therefore, magazines can often give you a better perspective on an issue. One downside of magazines is that their information can be dated because they are published less frequently than newspapers.

Many periodicals are specialized, addressing different kinds of issues in depth. A quick glance at the shelves in your local library or bookstore will reveal magazines that concentrate on politics, the environment, foreign policy, the economy, and so on. Each contains a wealth of articles on different aspects of the publication's focus. These specialized periodicals can be extremely valuable in researching your topic.

With so many magazines available, how will you decide which to read? One outstanding way to research periodicals is to use the *Reader's Guide to Periodical Literature*, found in your public library. This is an index that lists articles by subject headings, so you can easily search for articles relevant to your topic. Suppose that you were researching environmental policy. The entries in the *Reader's Guide* index might look like this:

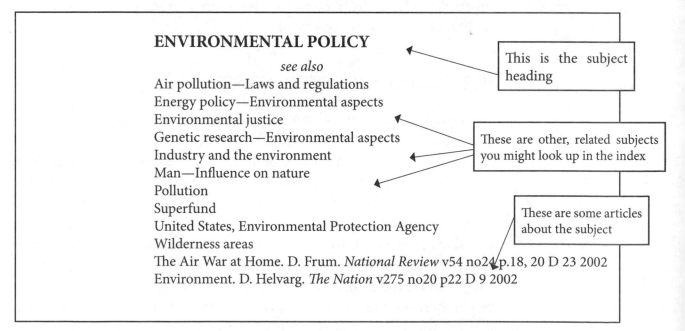

ENVIRONMENTAL POLICY

This is the subject heading

see also

Air pollution—Laws and regulations
Energy policy—Environmental aspects
Environmental justice
Genetic research—Environmental aspects
Industry and the environment
Man—Influence on nature
Pollution
Superfund
United States, Environmental Protection Agency
Wilderness areas

These are other, related subjects you might look up in the index

The Air War at Home. D. Frum. *National Review* v54 no24 p.18, 20 D 23 2002
Environment. D. Helvarg. *The Nation* v275 no20 p22 D 9 2002

These are some articles about the subject

How would you find one of the articles in the index? Remember that the index gives you only the bibliographical information about the article. Finding the actual article is up to you. If you were interested in learning more about air pollution in the United States, the first article in the short list above, "The Air War at Home," might be useful. Here is what the information in this entry means:

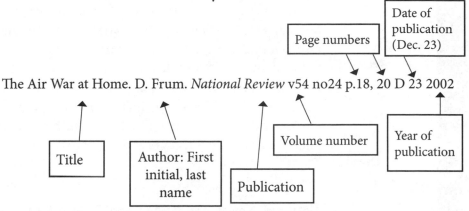

This information, called a *citation*, tells you everything you need to locate the article. Once you have found a promising citation, copy it and see if your library has the periodical in its list of holdings. Most libraries shelve their periodicals alphabetically and then by volume number. Go to the specific volume you need and find the issue number and the appropriate page. This process sounds complicated, but it isn't. If you get confused, just look for the year and the date of publication and forget about the volume and issue numbers. Many libraries also have the *Reader's Guide* in electronic form, in which case you may be able to access the full text of the article you seek from their computer.

Most school and public libraries list their materials on computer. These computer systems are easy to use, with help guides for age groups and reading levels. They are designed for students new to the library, in addition to those with advanced research skills. A library computer will have a catalog of all of the library's periodicals, reference works, books, videotapes, microfilm, and other materials. It may also offer one or more academic search services from which you access electronic versions of scholarly articles.

Many libraries have electronic resources called search services. You can use these to browse a variety of subjects, people, products, geographical locations, histories, and organizations. They are easy to use—just type in an author's name, a title, or a keyword, and the search service does the rest. Some search services have full text of national and international newspapers and magazine articles. Others will link you to Web sites on your research topic.

SOME ONLINE SERVICES

- **EBSCO, INFOTRAC, and PROQUEST**

  These services provide general reference information on people, places, and subjects, particularly social studies and language arts. INFOTRAC also offers a "Junior Edition," which is a periodical database designed for students in the middle grades. It includes a listing of full text articles from magazines and newspapers, as well as encyclopedia information, dictionary definitions, and maps. This search service concentrates on current events, popular culture, health, history, sports, arts, and sciences. There is also INFORME, a Spanish-language version of INFOTRAC.

- **National Newspaper Index and INFOTRAC Full Text Newspaper Collection**

  These services provide full text articles from daily newspapers. The National Newspaper Index keeps a record of all the news from five major national newspapers: the *Los Angeles Times, the New York Times, the Washington Post, the Christian Science Monitor*, and the *Wall Street Journal*. INFOTRAC lists fifty-six national and international newspapers, including those listed from the National Newspaper Index.

- **Opposing Viewpoints Resource Center**

  This site lists articles that argue the pros and cons of dozens of current events and debate topics. Topics include censorship, education, endangered species, environmental policy, health care reform, media violence, terrorism, trade, and welfare.

A popular example of a library search service is EBSCO Information Services, which accesses more than 100 databases and thousands of journals, including reference and other resources for students in the middle grades. The materials include newspapers, reports, magazines, almanacs, dictionaries, encyclopedias, public opinion polls, government information, maps, personal profiles, pamphlets, and the full text of books. There is also a current events database, examining political, social, economic, scientific, and cultural controversies.

The EBSCO search page for middle school students is known as Searchasaurus®. It is an easy and fun site to use and explore. You simply click on the picture of the object that you want to search. Are you interested in the research databases, which will give you access to books, magazines, newspapers, and reports? Click "Middle Search Plus." Do you need background information on a subject before beginning your research? Click on "General Encyclopedia."

If you click the "Middle School Plus" image, you will receive a screen that lets you make several decisions about your research. You can search only for full text articles. You can list a reading level, so that you receive only those articles that you can understand. You can select a particular subject area to examine, such as "U.S. History" or "Science."

Of course, you can also use EBSCO's expanded list of databases, which includes more resources, such as daily newspapers, academic journals, and government reports that are not written specifically for a middle-school audience. This on-line site is also easy to use. Just like the middle school page, you type in your search word, phrase, or several words; indicate whether you want full-text only results; and list a reading level. With the full database, you can also limit a search to a particular time period (for example, after January 1, 2004, or between November 2000 and March 2001).

The site is also available in Spanish and French.

Once you find your article, you can either copy or download it for future use or read it in the library. When you read the article, take notes. This will help you keep track of information as well as give you ideas for future research. As you read, record at least the following information:

- Article title
- Magazine title
- Date of publication (month, year, and date)
- Author's name
- Author's qualifications (Look at the beginning or end of the article for these. The magazine may also have a page at the front that introduces the authors in the issue.)
- Basic argument of the article, or the author's conclusion
- Reasons offered for that argument
- Evidence (including examples) offered to prove that argument
- Arguments offered against the major points of the article
- Other sources of information to research (Many articles will mention Web sites or other sources for further reading on the topic. Make sure you write these down!)

Organize your notes by subject. You will find it more useful if all of your information about handguns, for example, is in one place, rather than scattered among the various topics you may be researching. This organization will help you translate your research into effective arguments for debate.

SOME PERIODICALS OF INTEREST FOR YOUR RESEARCH

The Atlantic Monthly
Bulletin of the Atomic Scientists
Columbia Journalism Review
The Ecologist
The Economist
Extra!
Foreign Affairs
Foreign Policy
Harper's
In These Times
Mother Jones
The Nation
National Review
Newsweek
The New Yorker
Scientific American
Time
U.S. News & World Report
The Weekly Standard
Z

WHAT'S ON THE SHELF? USING BOOKS FOR RESEARCH

The most obvious place to do research is in books. Debaters find books extremely valuable because they examine the subject in more depth than magazines or newspapers. Book authors have more time to investigate and consider their subjects as well as more space in which to present their arguments and conclusions.

You might get more useful information, ideas for arguments, and evidence from reading one book than twenty magazine articles. However, books do have some disadvantages, particularly if you are researching current events. It can take many years to write a book. Preparing the book for publication also takes time because books must be edited, printed, marketed, and distributed. As a result, information in even very recently published books can be out of date. You should always supplement books with more up-to-date sources.

Your public library probably has a large collection of books on your topic. In addition, it can order books you might need from hundreds of other libraries through interlibrary loan. Libraries list their books either in a card catalog or a computer index. Normally the card catalog lists only books at that branch. A computer index may list books held by other libraries in the system.

To ensure that you find all the books you need, use different subject headings that might be relevant to your topic. Try brainstorming subjects related to your main topic. This will help you think of new keywords to broaden your search. For example, if you are researching "minimum wage," you might try other subject headings like "working conditions" and "labor policy." You can find additional keywords in the *Library of Congress Subject Headings Guide*, which is available at most libraries. Here is an example for the listing for "Free choice of employment":

      Civil rights

      Employment, free choice of

      Freedom of employment

      Freedom of occupation

      Labor supply

      Liberty of employment

      Liberty of occupation

      Occupation, liberty of

Each keyword search will produce different magazine and newspaper articles, books, and Web sites for your topic research.

You will need citation information to find your book. This includes the title of the book, and the name of the author. You can use this information to find the book's call number so that you can locate it on the library shelf. Write down the book's citation and call number before you go to the shelves so that you can ask the librarian for help if you cannot find the book.

Do not just grab your book and leave. Because books are organized by subject, you may find others of interest around your target book. Take a minute to look at these. If the titles seem interesting, glance at their table of contents. See if the chapter titles appear useful. If so, you might take an additional book or two with you for further reading. Some of the best "finds" in libraries happen by browsing the shelves. This browsing technique also works for magazines and journals. If you find a magazine that seems particularly useful, look through other issues to see if they contain helpful articles.

Many debaters avoid using books for research because they think it will take too long to read them. While reading an entire book takes time, you can gather the information you need quickly. Start with a clear idea of what you are looking for. If you are researching the minimum wage, for example, you may want arguments for and against increasing the minimum wage. You might also be interested in the history of the topic because it can provide background on the consequences of increasing the minimum wage.

When you first open a book, note the publication date, which appears on the copyright page, just after the title page. Is the book recent? Then note the author's qualifications. Does the author have an advanced degree? In what field? Has the author written other books, especially other books on this subject? Often, books will have an "about the author" page at the back. If not, look at the dust jacket. If you cannot find the author's qualifications in the book, try using Google or another Internet search engine to find out more about him. Include the name of the book, its publication date, and the name and qualifications of the author in your research notebook.

Next, look at the table of contents. In many cases, examining the chapter headings can tell you a lot about what is in a book. If you were to come across the table of contents below, what would you expect to find in the book? What would you not expect to find? What might you expect to find in each chapter?

Chapter 1: History of the Death Penalty in the United States

Chapter 2: Why Does Punishment Matter?

Chapter 3: The Movement Against the Death Penalty

Chapter 4: Efforts to Reform the Death Penalty

Chapter 5: Portrait of a Reformer

Chapter 6: Conflicts Between the States and the Federal Government

If you were researching the death penalty, this book would have lots of good information for both sides of the issue. Remember that you are looking for arguments and evidence both pro and con as well as background information. Thus you would most likely find chapters 1, 2, 3, 4, 7, and 8 useful. You cannot tell from the table of contents whether you need to look through chapters 5 and 6. Next, examine the index (found at the end of the text), which lists each major issue, person, or event mentioned in the book. Look through it for subject headings that are relevant to your research project and read what the author has to say on the indicated pages. Then decide if you should read more of the book.

This imaginary book is clearly helpful for your research. But what about other books whose value is not apparent from the table of contents or index? In these cases, read the conclusion first. It will give you a sense of the strength of the author's arguments and evidence, the breadth and depth of her research, and the overall relevance of the book. If the conclusion seems promising, read the chapters that look useful. Remember to keep good notes in your research notebook. You never know when you will have to debate the same subject twice, and the notes will come in handy the second time.

Do not forget to examine reference books that might help your research. Many reference guides—encyclopedias, biographical and geographical dictionaries, handbooks, and almanacs—provide background information, offer historical and current examples, and make your research more efficient. Always have a dictionary handy to help explain unfamiliar words.

GOING ONLINE: RESEARCHING ON THE INTERNET

The Internet and the World Wide Web are important sources of information of all kinds. The Web has dramatically increased the availability of information that might not have been accessible to the average person just a few years ago. However, this advantage is also one of its biggest drawbacks. The Web simply contains too much information, and often you cannot tell what is accurate or best. After all, anyone can publish anything on the Web, and most Web sites do not have editors who check facts.

Nevertheless, if you make smart use of the World Wide Web, you will find it a fast and effective way to research. You probably have some experience navigating the Web. You may know, for example, that every Web site has a location or address known as an "URL" (this stands for Universal Record Locator). Some URLs are very basic. For example, the *Los Angeles Times* is found online at http://www.latimes.com. The full URL of an address normally begins with http://www. Suffixes (at the end of addresses) tell you something about the site or identify the country in which the host computer is located. The chart below presents some common suffixes.

.com	A commercial Web site
.edu	The Web site of a school, often a university or college
.k12	A school site
.org	Usually (but not necessarily) the site of a nonprofit organization
.gov	A government Web site
.net	A personal page or a commercial page
.(state).us	A site used by state or local governments
~(name)	A personal page
/members	A personal page
.uk	A site from the United Kingdom

SEARCH ENGINES

A search engine produces a list of Web sites based on keywords found in the sites. The majority of popular search engines work by sending out a spider or crawler to fetch as many documents as possible. Spiders and crawlers are electronic signals that visit Web sites, read the information on the site, and return the information to a central database. Crawlers will return to Web sites on a regular basis to examine any updates. A search engine uses the data in its central file to index information by keyword. When you type a keyword into a search engine, it shows you a listing of the popular Web sites and documents that include the keyword. In other words, you are not actually searching the World Wide Web; you are searching an index compiled from Web sites.

Because you are not searching the current Web, your search may return old and outdated links. In addition, because different search engines use different types of crawlers to gather information and a variety of mathematical formulas to index it, searching different engines may produce different results. Therefore, you should use more than one search engine to complete your research.

A poorly constructed search can return too many hits (potential results) to be useful. To research efficiently, use Boolean operators— AND, NOT, OR, EXCEPT or other words and symbols—to limit your search. Each search engine will explain which terms and symbols to use on its site. In Alta Vista and Lycos, for example, you use "+" for AND and "-" for NOT. In most other engines, you use AND, NOT, and OR to get your results.

For example, if you are searching for information on a particular kind of vehicle, you might search for:

"car or automobile"

This would ensure that you would receive hits for either word.

If you wanted to limit or eliminate some hits, you might enter:

"New York" not "New York state"

The quotation marks show that you are searching for the exact phrase. You are searching for "New York" rather than a Web site that has both the words "new" and "York." Thus, you avoid a hit from a site describing a "new" building in "York," England. By typing *not* "New York state," your search will exclude sites with this phrase.

MAJOR SEARCH ENGINES

- www.altavista.com
- www.excite.com
- www.go.com
- www.google.com
- www.hotbot.com
- www.infoseek.com
- www.lycos.com
- www.profusion.com
- www.webcrawler.com
- www.yahoo.com

Most people get frustrated searching the Web because they come up with too many hits. Try these tips to avoid the problem:

- Take a few minutes to think about what you want to get out of the search before you start. For example, if your topic were school uniforms, you might want to research arguments for and against wearing them. You will also need evidence for these claims.

- When you want to search for a specific phrase, put it in quotes. For example, if you were looking for evidence that wearing school uniforms is beneficial, you might search for the phrase "benefits of school uniforms" rather than typing in the individual words. This strategy works best with search engines like Google, which index the contents of Web pages as well as their titles.

- Use the bookmark function of your Web browser to mark sites to which you might return. This will make your search more efficient. If you are sharing a computer, do not forget to erase your bookmarks when you are finished.

EVALUATING WEB SITES

You must critically evaluate the Web sites you use in your research. Be aware of the purpose of the site you have accessed. Some are used to sell products; others are designed to entertain. Still others advocate for ideas or simply present information. Knowing the purpose of the site will help you evaluate the information in it.

One good way to evaluate Web or any other information is to find out what the source is. Ask yourself if the source is biased. A biased source has a stake in whether or not you believe the information. For example, if PepsiCo were to design a commercial telling you that Pepsi tastes great, would you automatically accept its claim? No, because you know that PepsiCo is biased. The company has a financial stake in whether or not you believe the information.

Note that a bias is not the same as a preference. Everyone has preferences. For example, you may prefer a certain kind of music, flavor of ice cream, or style of clothing. Does that mean that you cannot be trusted to talk about music, ice cream, or clothing? Of course not. You are skeptical of biased sources because you don't believe they will present all the facts fairly (or at all).

Here are some questions you can ask to help you determine if a source is biased:

- Who is responsible for the information?

- Does the author have a reason to distort or change the information?

- Does the author (a person or an organization) have a membership in another organization that might influence the information?

- Is the author trying to persuade you to adopt his beliefs?

One final tip for Internet research: Keep looking. You may be tempted to stop after you have found one or two promising sites, but this is a mistake. Consult a wide variety of sites to ensure that your information is fair and balanced.

MOVING ON: RESEARCHING USING YOUR AGENDA

As you research, sort your findings into proposition claims (arguments for the debate motion) and opposition claims (arguments against the motion). One good way to do this is to devote a page in your research notebook to each side of the topic. You then can document your information under the appropriate heading. Many of the facts you find will be irrelevant to debate research. If you know a fact is irrelevant, do not write it down. Sometimes you cannot immediately determine if a fact is relevant or not. In this case, start an "Other" page in your notebook so you can jot these items down and sort them later.

As you engage in more debates, you will become a better researcher because you will be more familiar with what kinds of information you need to succeed. Not all information is equally valuable. Its value depends on how you plan to use it. Suppose you are researching the issue of school uniforms. After some investigation, you find a study that claims uniforms do not reduce school violence. You might not know immediately how you can use this information, but you include it in your notebook. As you research, think about what major arguments you want to make on each side of the motion. Once you discover that some people say that school uniforms reduce school violence, you then realize that the study you noted is an argument for the opposition side.

As you research, fill out an ARE chart for each side of the motion:

Proposition	Opposition
Major Argument 1 Assertion: Reasoning: Evidence:	*Major Argument 1* Assertion: Reasoning: Evidence:
Major Argument 2 Assertion: Reasoning: Evidence:	*Major Argument 2* Assertion: Reasoning: Evidence:
Major Argument 3 Assertion: Reasoning: Evidence:	*Major Argument 3* Assertion: Reasoning: Evidence:

Although these charts can help organize your research, you must be more flexible in a debate than the charts suggest. For example, you must answer the arguments of the other side—not merely make your own. Still, outlining arguments for both sides will give you a good idea of what major arguments might be made in the debate.

As you conduct more in-depth research on the issue, ask yourself the following questions:

- Who is involved?

- Where are they?

- What are they doing?

- Why are they doing that?

- Is that a good thing or a bad thing?

- How do/did they react to doing that?

You may not be able to answer all of these questions all of the time, but they are a good place to start. They will help you identify the significant elements of the issue and determine what major arguments both sides could make.

SUGGESTED EXERCISES

Keyword Search

Use the *Library of Congress Subject Headings Guide* and the Internet to find keywords for the term *climatology*. Make a list of the keywords and phrases that might help you research the issue of global warming and climate change. Submit the keywords to several Internet search engines and examine the results. Did you find helpful information about the topic?

Library Scavenger Hunt

Use the school or public library to find the following materials or information. You must use a variety of materials and search terms to succeed.

- A dictionary of environmental terms
- The complete text of the Fourteenth Amendment to the U.S. Constitution
- Two political quotations describing the value of democracy
- The unemployment rate and number of people unemployed in the United States
- A major historical event in the Middle East in the 1970s
- The number of students in the United States who do not graduate from high school
- An argument opposing human space exploration
- The country with the lowest infant mortality
- The number of Electoral College votes needed to be elected president
- The number of annual deaths from handguns, automobiles, and toys in the United States
- Substitute terms for *inaction* from a thesaurus
- An important news event on April 22, 1997
- The change in the price of gold from 1980 to today
- The members of the North Atlantic Treaty Organization (NATO)
- An argument in favor of raising gasoline taxes

SECTION III
DEBATING IN CLASS AND COMPETITION

Once you have learned the basics of public speaking, argumentation, and research, it is time to participate in debate. You already know the basics of the three vs. three Middle School Public Debate Program format. You may also learn many other kinds of debating activities. This section will help you refine your debating skills and help you prepare for debate competitions and classroom debates.

Debating is like any skill—it requires practice. If you are learning to play a musical instrument, you have to practice regularly. Even then, you must work for years to attain proficiency. Learning to debate is like learning to play a musical instrument—you must work hard and practice the necessary skills.

CHAPTER 7

MAKING ARGUMENTS MATTER: IMPACTS

SUCCESSFUL

debaters are able to show why their arguments matter. They can explain the significance of arguments in a way that makes them important and real. Both sides present many arguments in a debate. How will you or the judges determine which are the most important?

WHAT'S AN IMPACT?

One way to evaluate arguments is by looking at their significance. In debate, an argument's significance is called its *impact*. To debate effectively, you must learn how to weigh impacts. You must be able to say that your team's arguments matter most and give reasons for your assertion.

Do not assume that you, the judge, and the other debaters agree on what arguments are important. In debates, you often may make an argument that you think is important, but the other team and perhaps the judge do not. This frequently happens because you have not explained adequately why your argument matters.

You must follow your arguments with a "therefore" statement providing reasons why they matter. For example, merely saying, "Children should watch less television because it affects them negatively," is not enough. You must say how watching too much television affects them and how many children are affected. Explaining your impacts shows the judge and the audience the significance of your issue and the importance of your argument.

EXPLAINING YOUR IMPACTS

Explain why your arguments matter—what impacts they have. To win debates consistently, you must appeal to both reason and emotions.

Sometimes debaters fail to explain their impacts in a way that makes them tangible to the judge. It is not enough, for example, to say that your proposal is a good idea because it gets people out of poverty, helps the economy, cleans up the air, or even because nine out of ten dentists endorse it. To make an impact persuasive, you must flesh it out. Personalize it. Help the judge visualize the potential consequences of the issue in a way that makes it important and meaningful. Judges like to vote for ideas that seem realistic and beneficial. In this way, they are like people who want to purchase products that they are certain will solve an immediate problem. If you understand this element of judge psychology, you will make your arguments more persuasive.

Most debates are won or lost on good impact explanation and comparison. For example, you could say: "Our proposal is good because it brings people out of poverty." Or, you could say:

> Hundreds of thousands of people, many of them children, are starving or malnourished in our country because of serious poverty, and few of them have any hope of surviving to make a meaningful life for themselves. Imagine what it is like to live with inadequate food, no shelter, poor clothing, constantly wracked by disease. Then, imagine what a tremendous help our proposal for reform would be. Increasing welfare would give poor families a real chance at life and would, over time, improve and protect millions and millions of lives by lifting a whole segment of society out of poverty.

The speaker uses a variety of persuasive techniques to make her argument more tangible. What are some of the "power words" she uses? What is her strategy for persuading the judge?

If you have trouble explaining your impacts, think in terms of because. Begin with an impact claim like this one: "The loss of the ozone layer is bad." Then expand on it by using a series of "because" statements:

> The loss of the ozone layer is bad…because…more UV radiation will reach the surface of the Earth, and that's bad…because…many people will get skin cancer as a result, and that's bad…because…skin cancer is often fatal, and the incidence of skin cancer will increase as UV intensity increases.

Remember, judges like to vote on issues that seem important and tangible.

SUGGESTED EXERCISES

Impacts

Explain why each of the following impacts is bad.

- drought
- crime
- failing a class
- famine
- floods
- forest fires
- global warming
- imprisonment
- inequality
- losing the freedom of speech
- sexism
- slavery

COMPARING YOUR IMPACTS

Once you have learned how to show why your issues matter, you must develop the ability to compare your arguments to those of your opponents. Remember that debate is not just about making arguments. It is also about answering those from the other side and showing why your arguments beat theirs. One way to do this is to compare relative costs and benefits. Another is to compare relative impacts. Say that you are debating whether the United States should lower the voting age. The proposition side argues that lowering the voting age will be good because it will help children become full citizens and encourage their participation in democracy. The opposition argues that letting children vote will be bad because they are irresponsible and will make bad electoral decisions. How could you compare these two arguments?

Weighing Arguments

In order to win the debate, you must compare the impacts, or consequences, of each position. Sometimes we call this method *weighing* the impacts, because debaters use a mental scale to determine whose arguments are more important and why. Using the "because" method you learned in the previous section, you might explain why each issue was important.

> **Proposition speaker:** Better training for democracy is important, *because otherwise* children will grow up not knowing how to participate as good citizens, and that's important, *because* these children will then make bad electoral decisions all their lives, and that's important, *because* then our country will elect candidates who will also make bad decisions, like going to war or wrecking the economy, which would be bad, *because* then millions of people will have trouble paying rent and feeding their children.

The example above shows how the proposition team might explain the impacts of their arguments. They are saying that the judge should vote to lower the voting age because otherwise we will not have good citizenship training, and that, in turn, might have very serious consequences. Now let's look at how the opposition might phrase their impact statement:

> **Opposition speaker:** Lowering the voting age will be harmful, *because*…children will make bad choices when voting. For example, they will be manipulated by peer pressure, or they will make decisions based on silly things. This will be bad, *because*…they will not learn the importance of voting and will probably not vote later in life, because they will not see it as a responsibility. This will be bad, *because*…without high voter turnout, special interests will find it easier to manipulate elections, which is bad *because*…then we will elect candidates who are not responsible to the people and who will not make decisions in the people's interest.

Whose argument is more substantial? Which speaker makes the consequences of his issue more tangible? How does he do that? If you had to weigh these two arguments, which would be the more significant? How would you compare the two?

All debates are about comparing arguments and impacts. The items below illustrate some of the most effective techniques you can use to show that your arguments have substantial impact:

- **Number of people affected.** This is one of the simplest impact yardsticks you can use. To say that some things affect more people than others seems basic, yet debaters often forget to mention this. If your proposal will save millions of lives by preventing war, pestilence, famine, or plague, then you should stress this. For example, if you were arguing that children should watch less television, you might contend that TV violence potentially affects millions of American children.

- **Significance of the harm.** By itself, the number of people affected is not an adequate measure of impact. You also must show what happens to these people. Is the impact significant? If you were arguing that children should watch less television so that they would be exposed to less violence, you would need to explain why exposure to TV violence is bad—for example, because it may encourage children to commit violent acts.

- **Probability and risk.** You cannot simply assess the size of an impact or consequence. You must also consider the probability of the consequence. Is it likely to occur? We consider probability all the time. For example, we decide to cross the street every day despite the possibility that a bus might run us over. We make this decision because we think the probability of such an accident is low. Risk is a very important concept in assessing impact. If you can show that a particular consequence is very likely, you will boost the significance of your argument. Or, if you can show that the consequences the other team has presented are unlikely, you will help your side.

- **Ethics and morality.** In some debates, one team may argue that there is an ethical or moral imperative to vote for their side of the motion. Suppose that the proposition team defends a case that demands an end to racial profiling. They argue that profiling should be stopped because it is a violation of human and constitutional rights. The opposition team argues that a ban on racial profiling will limit the ability of law enforcement agencies to fight crime and terrorism, leading to loss of life and property. How should we compare these impacts? A smart proposition team will argue that the end does not justify the means. They may say that the government's obligation to protect civil rights is an ethical obligation.

Whatever techniques you use, you must practice comparing issues and their consequences. With practice, you will find that comparison becomes easier. You will win more debates by engaging the arguments of the other side and showing that yours are more important, because…

SUGGESTED EXERCISES

Competing Impacts

Below are several pairs of competing impacts. Compare them using the techniques above. Pick one of the pair and show why it is more important than its companion impact. Then show how the other impact is more important. Do not forget to make your arguments tangible and significant. Try starting your statement with a sentence like this: "Earthquakes are worse than floods, because…." Once you have finished making this comparison, try it the other way: "Floods are worse than earthquakes, because…."

- a bad haircut vs. a bad outfit
- cheating on a test vs. lying to your parents
- earthquakes vs. flooding
- economic recession vs. environmental ruin
- losing $100 vs. losing $1,000
- losing an arm vs. losing a leg
- tornado vs. tidal wave
- warfare vs. poverty
- water pollution vs. air pollution

CHAPTER 8:
OPPOSITION STRATEGIES

THIS chapter will help you improve your skills when you are the opposition. Many students have difficulty learning how to debate on the opposition side because they do not know what the proposition side will say. These kinds of speaking situations occur all the time. You do not have a lot of preparation time before important conversations with friends, family, or teachers. If your principal wants to meet with you, she does not send you notes about what she will say weeks in advance. You will encounter similar situations throughout your life. Participating in debate trains you to think on your feet.

You already have learned the basic responsibilities for opposition speakers in a debate. The proposition team tries to prove a case for the motion. The opposition's job is to show that the judge should not vote for the proposition's case. There are several ways they can accomplish this.

REFUTING THE CASE

First and foremost, you must refute the case. The opposition team should not leave the proposition's arguments untouched. You may be tempted to present only your own arguments, but you must clash with the proposition, if only to show that your arguments are more important, take theirs into account, or otherwise make their case irrelevant. You must refute their major arguments using good reasoning and counter-examples. Make sure that you take good notes on your flowsheet so that you can answer the proposition's case.

If you are the first opposition speaker, your job is to make arguments against the case that your partners can extend. They will contribute their own examples and ideas, but your initial refutation will set the stage for their speeches.

Make sure that you deal with all the proposition's major arguments. Do not address every point they made in their opening speech; instead, determine which arguments seem most important. This is not always easy. Beginning debaters usually go to one extreme or the other. Either they answer none of the case or they respond to each point, failing to make any arguments of their own. The only way to evaluate the importance of arguments is to practice. Over time, you will develop a better sense of what is most important, regardless of the side you are on.

How do you know which arguments matter most? You must learn to distinguish between relevant and irrelevant information. Reading and studying novels and short stories has already taught you how to do this. Some parts of a story are relevant to its outcome, and some are not. For example, in the story of Hansel and Gretel, the two children eventually push the witch into the oven and escape. In telling the story, the author provided details to give you a feeling for setting and place. These could be changed easily, while the story's outcome remains the same. Some of the information in the story is relevant, and some is not.

In debates, the proposition's case functions like a story. The point of the story is that the motion for debate is more likely to be true than false. Some of the issues in the proposition's case may be relevant to proving this; others may be less important or irrelevant. In the speech below, the speaker is making the case for increasing public transportation. As you read the excerpt, note which information is relevant to the conclusion and which is not.

> Our community should substantially increase public transportation because we now have very little. Everyone has to drive. As a result, the traffic is bad, and people are late to work. The other day, I had to work late because I could not get to my job on time. When I got home, my dinner was cold. Also, air pollution is increasing because there are so many cars on the street. Air pollution is very dangerous and can cause breathing problems in children. It is a big problem all over the world. Finally, public transportation would reduce costs for all our residents. People would not need cars because they could take the train. The town would not have to build roads. Plus, the town is slow building new roads anyway. This is why we should have public transportation.

The speaker is making a case for increasing public transportation. She offers three major points:

- Public transportation will reduce traffic.
- Public transportation will reduce air pollution.
- Public transportation will reduce costs for everyone.

She also provides additional information, including reasons for these three points. Nevertheless, the speech contains information that is not clearly related to her major points. For example, she says that traffic problems make people late to work. This explains the consequences of traffic, which is important for making the speaker's case, but she then goes on to say, "The other day, I had to work late because I could not get to my job on time. When I got home, my dinner was cold." She does not explain how this is relevant to the case. In fact, she does not even show that her lateness was related to traffic problems. Perhaps she just slept in!

Later, the speaker makes the point that public transportation will reduce air pollution. She maintains that air pollution is bad because it causes breathing problems in children. She then says that air pollution is a big problem all over the world. Even if this is true, she does not show how the point helps her case. This is an example of irrelevant information.

A final example of irrelevant information comes during the speaker's last major point. She says that public transportation will reduce costs for everyone, and shows how this might be true because the town will not have to build roads. This is a good way to show a reduction in costs, but she then says that the town is very slow in building roads. This is not important to the larger issue: whether the town should increase public transportation.

To refute the proposition team's case effectively, you must know which of the many points they make are relevant to their proof of the motion. You must make sure that you refute all of their important points. Usually you can tell if an argument is important because the following is true:

- **It is more significant.** As you now know, some arguments are more significant than others, because of either the number of people involved or the extent to which they are affected. You need to address these issues, if only to say that they are not significant.

- **It is related to several other arguments in the debate.** You must address an argument that is related to many others. By doing so, you answer several of your opponent's points with one stroke. For example, you might debate a team that claims that their proposal to increase taxes will increase jobs. They might then have six arguments about why increasing jobs would be good. If you diagram this argument, it would look like this:

Increasing Taxes ⟶ Increased jobs ⟶ Benefits 1, 2, 3, 4, 5 & 6

If you could remove the link between increasing taxes and increasing jobs, perhaps by proving that increasing taxes does not lead to job growth, you would also eliminate all six benefits. Better still, you might be able to show that increasing taxes decreases jobs. This would allow you to turn their argument to your side.

All opposition speakers must try to neutralize the proposition's case. You must counter and minimize the proposition's claims to convince the judge that their case is weak.

MAKING OFFENSIVE ARGUMENTS

You cannot win debates or sporting contests merely by playing defense. You must take the offense. In debates, a *defensive argument* is an argument that shows why a certain point does not lose you the debate. You do a thorough job of refuting the case because you want to play good defense against the proposition team's major points. But this is not enough. You must also make *offensive arguments*. These are reasons why you think you should win the debate. They show why the proposition's case (or a key part of it) is not only wrong, but also bad or dangerous.

Below are examples of the two types of argument. Each includes a sample quote from a speaker and two potential responses, one defensive and one offensive. As you read them, think about the difference between the two.

Example 1

Speaker: The United States should ban research on human cloning. Human cloning is not ethical, and a ban would stop this dangerous and immoral research.

Defense: Banning cloning research would not stop it. Companies and scientists will just go to other countries.

Offense: Banning cloning research will drive research into unregulated laboratories and to foreign countries. It will make the problem worse, because governments will not be able to control how research is conducted.

In Example 1, the defensive argument says that the speaker's proposal would not solve the problem. It argues that the proposal is not good enough. The offensive argument asserts that the proposal will make the problem worse. It argues that the proposition team's position is dangerous.

Example 2

Speaker: Children who commit violent crimes should go to adult prisons. This is the best way to keep our streets safe. Violent criminals should not get special treatment just because they are children.

Defense: Putting children in adult prisons will not solve our crime problem. Young criminals need help, not punishment.

Offense: Putting children in adult prisons will only increase our crime problem. When children are sent to adult prisons, they learn how to commit other crimes and become more dangerous.

Example 2 illustrates that sometimes it is best to make both defensive and offensive arguments. In Example 1, the offensive argument was basically a stronger version of the defensive. In Example 2, the two arguments are different. The opposition says that young criminals need help, not severe punishment, and that adult prisons will make the problem worse.

Example 3

Speaker: Schools should be able to censor school newspapers. The principal or teachers should have the final say over what is included because some issues are just too controversial to publish. Students can't make good judgments about this.

Defense: Censoring school newspapers won't suppress ideas. Teachers, students, and parents will still talk about issues, even if they are not published.

Offense: Censoring school newspapers won't suppress ideas. Teachers, students, and parents will still talk about issues. Censorship can lead to unsubstantiated rumors and gossip. If ideas are published in the school newspaper, they can be discussed openly. Censorship won't help stop the spread of controversial ideas, but may make the situation worse.

In Example 3, the offensive argument is an extension of the defensive argument. The defensive argument says that censoring newspapers will not stop the spread of controversial ideas. The offensive argument takes this a step further and shows why censorship might make things worse.

An offensive argument shows why your side should win the debate. The opposition uses these arguments to explain why the proposition team's proposal is harmful or dangerous. When you say that the proposal is likely to make the problem worse, increase problems, have more costs than benefits, or have more disadvantages than advantages, you are making offensive arguments.

SUGGESTED EXERCISES

Name that problem!

Develop one offensive argument against each proposal listed below. To do so, you must come up with one problem that the proposal might create and show a negative result of the problem. Here's an example:

> **Proposal:** There is too much logging in American forests. We should ban all logging so that we can preserve our trees.
>
> **Problem:** If we ban all logging, the timber industry will collapse because there's no work for loggers.
>
> **Result:** Millions will be out of work and live in poverty, unable to feed their families or pay rent.

Remember that there is no right answer for these exercises; a proposal might cause a number of problems. If you have trouble coming up with a problem, use your issue analysis skills to think about these questions: Who's involved? Why are they involved? Who would the proposal affect?

> **a. Proposal:** American children have too many cavities. We must stop selling candy bars to children under eighteen. This will help children have fewer cavities and better teeth.
>
> **b. Proposal:** Atlantastan has developed nuclear weapons. We should invade that country and remove the weapons. This will prevent Atlantastan from using them.
>
> **c. Proposal:** Students at our school are having trouble learning math. We should introduce a daily school-wide math test. This will ensure that all children are learning math.
>
> **d. Proposal:** The air in our community is too polluted. We must ban

single-occupancy vehicles. Everyone must car-pool. Fewer cars on the road will reduce air pollution.

e. Proposal: Handguns cause too many deaths. We should make handguns illegal. Doing so will mean fewer deaths from gun violence each year.

f. Proposal: Political candidates take too much money from special interests. As a result, interest groups have too much influence over politics. We should stop all groups from giving money to campaigns. This will mean that candidates can use only individual donations and their own money in elections.

g. Proposal: Children watch too much violence on television. We must make sure that networks do not show violent programs before midnight. This will mean that children will not see violence on television.

OFF-CASE ARGUMENTS AND INDIRECT REFUTATION

You must make offensive arguments to win a debate. You cannot say merely that the other side is not good enough. You have to explain why voting for the other side could be harmful. Sometimes your offensive arguments will be related directly to those the proposition presents. On other occasions, you may be able to indicate an important problem that is only indirectly related to the proposition case. In still other situations, you may need to introduce issues they did not mention to point out problems with their case.

Let's look at a few examples. Perhaps you are debating the topic "Middle schools should require students to wear uniforms." The proposition team presents several points to support their case. They might say that school uniforms save money, that they reduce the teasing of students who cannot afford new clothes, and that they decrease violence because students cannot wear gang clothing. One issue that the proposition team has not mentioned is that of freedom of expression. You might argue that requiring uniforms prevents students from expressing their individuality. This issue is not directly mentioned in the proposition's case, but it could be important. If you were to introduce it, you would be indirectly refuting the case. You would be telling the judge not to vote for school uniforms because wearing them restricts freedom of expression.

Here is another example of the same kind of argument. Say you are debating the topic "It is unethical to eat meat." The proposition's case says that we have an ethical obligation to protect the rights of all creatures, and so we should agree that eating meat is unethical. You might raise a different point: If we agree that it is unethical to eat meat, we are also agreeing that it is unethical to use animals for any purpose, including for scientific experimentation. You might say that we need to use animals for scientific experiments, because in so doing we can save millions of lives through testing vaccines and other medical treatments. The proposition team did not raise this issue, but it may be important for deciding who wins the debate. If you were to bring it up, you would be indirectly refuting the case.

Feel free to bring up issues or arguments of your own—arguments that are not mentioned by the other side, but that you think are relevant to the case. Sometimes, these indirect refutations are called **off-case** arguments, in contrast to **on-case** arguments, which directly refute the case. When you take notes in a debate, put off-case arguments on a separate piece of paper. These arguments will be disputed just like any others, but since they do not directly refute the case, they should not be placed next to it. In addition to your standard flowsheet, you might have another that looks like this for use in flowing "off-case" arguments:

1st Opposition Constructive	2nd Proposition Constructive	2nd Opp/Opp Rebuttal	Prop Rebuttal

You can see that this specialized flowsheet is designed to track arguments that began in the first opposition constructive (or even later in the debate).

If you completed the "Name that Problem!" exercise in the previous section of this chapter, you have probably come up with lots of off-case arguments of your own. There is nothing magic about them. The label is just a convenient way to help debaters organize their ideas so that they know which arguments directly and indirectly reply to the case.

One important type of off-case argument is called a *disadvantage*. A disadvantage is an argument that shows a harmful consequence of agreeing with the proposition. Most people argue disadvantages all the time:

Speaker 1: We should eat at the International House of Malaria.

Speaker 2: If we eat there, we'll get sick and possibly die.

Speaker 3: Let's sneak into a movie.

Speaker 4: If we get caught, we'll get in big trouble.

Speaker 5: I'm going to vote for Susie for class president.

Speaker 6: If Susie wins the election, she's going to cancel lunch.

In addition to presenting disadvantages, you might also show what opportunities are lost by agreeing with the case. Economists say that every action has at least one *opportunity* cost, the opportunity you lose by taking a specific course of action. For example, when you took the bus on Wednesday, you lost the opportunity to walk or ride your bike to school. These were the opportunity costs of your decision to use the bus. Or, when you ate at a particular restaurant, you chose not to eat at another. You traded one option for another. Every decision has opportunity costs.

Sometimes the opposition team will present opportunity costs. They may say that the judge should not vote for the proposition team's proposal because they have a better solution. They are then saying, "Don't do that, do this instead," just as you might say, "Let's eat at Restaurant B instead of Restaurant A." Let's look at how the opposition might use opportunity cost. If the proposition team said that the United States should lower the voting age to fourteen, the opposition team might say that the United States should lower the voting age to sixteen because most students have had a class in U.S. government by that age.

When the opposition team points out an opportunity cost of adopting the proposition's case, they are presenting a reason to reject the proposal. Because of this, the two proposals must be competitive. You should not be able to do both. If you could, one would not be the opportunity cost of the other. What if the proposition team said that the United States should lower the voting age to fourteen, and the opposition team countered that the United States should send a mission to Mars? The opportunity to go to Mars is not lost by lowering the voting age. These two options are not competitive, and so going to Mars is not a reason to reject the original proposal.

Make sure that the opportunity cost you raise is genuinely competitive with and better than the proposal. You can do this by showing that doing both the proposal and the lost opportunity would be a bad idea. For example, you could eat at both Restaurant A and Restaurant B, but doing so might give you a stomach ache and empty your wallet. Thus, the options are competitive. You must choose one.

SUGGESTED EXERCISES

Lost opportunities

Name an opportunity cost for each proposal below and explain why that lost opportunity would be competitive with the original proposal. You must explain why you cannot do both, or why doing both would be bad. Here's an example:

> **Proposal:** We should spend Saturday at the mall.
>
> **Opportunity Cost:** We should spend Saturday at the library.
>
> **It's competitive because:** If we spend Saturday at the mall, we can't spend Saturday at the library, and we will learn more if we spend Saturday at the library.

a. **Proposal:** You should spend your allowance on a new stereo.

b. **Proposal:** We should spend $100 million to go to Mars.

c. **Proposal:** We should not allow middle school students to take any elective classes. (HINT: The proposal says "any." Can you think of some good elective classes that should be allowed?)

d. **Proposal:** Our state should ban the sale of all SUVs. (HINT: "all"?)

CHAPTER 9:
THE DEBATE COMPETITION

ATTENDING

debate competitions is one of the most exciting parts of debating. At a competition, called a *tournament*, you will meet people from other schools and debate different issues. You will be evaluated by parent, community, high school, and college judges. You will receive comments from judges that will help you in future debates and have the opportunity to win awards for individual, team, and school performance. In short, you will always leave a debate competition a better debater.

You may be nervous before a debate competition. This is normal. Most people are afraid to speak in public, and merely attending a tournament is an act of courage. You should be proud of your abilities and your preparation. This chapter explains what you can expect and how to get the most out of the tournament experience. Remember that a tournament is like a science laboratory. It is an opportunity for you to practice what you have learned and to improve your skills.

BEFORE THE TOURNAMENT

You will be debating on a team of three people. You may choose your team, or your teacher or coach might assign you to one. Just as you are part of a team of three, you are also part of a team from your school. It is important to cooperate with your teammates and the rest of your school's debaters.

Make sure to discuss with your partners all the issues you will be debating. Coordinated preparation will pay off at a competition. Your school may have just a few or quite a lot of students on the debate team. Because all of you are representing your school, it is important to share information. When the topics for an upcoming competition are announced, you should work as a group to organize your research and preparation. This will make preparation more effective. One way to make preparation efficient is to have small groups work on each of the pre-announced topics. These groups can then share their notes and ideas with the entire team. Small groups can produce issue briefs with arguments for and against each of the topics, which they can photocopy for distribution to the rest of the club. Although you cannot use the actual briefs in debates, you will learn from the work of your fellow teammates, and you may use these briefs in your preparation time.

AT THE TOURNAMENT

If you have never attended a debate tournament, you may not know what to expect. Most tournaments will release a schedule in advance of the event. It may look like this:

Registration: 8:00-9:00

Round 1: 9:00

Round 2: 10:00

Round 3: 11:00

Lunch: 12-1:15

Round 4: 1:15

Round 5: 2:45

Awards: 4:15

Buses depart: 4:45

What does this schedule mean? Registration is the time when everyone arrives at the tournament. People will come in buses and cars from all over your area. Their coaches will check in with the tournament director. During this period, find a quiet place to work with your teammates for the upcoming debates. At 9:00, the tournament director will post a *pairing*. The pairing sheet tells students where they will be debating, what side they will take, and who their judge will be. The pairing sheet will look like this:

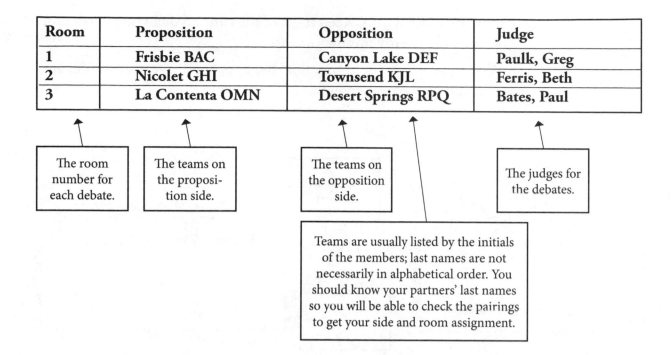

Room	Proposition	Opposition	Judge
1	Frisbie BAC	Canyon Lake DEF	Paulk, Greg
2	Nicolet GHI	Townsend KJL	Ferris, Beth
3	La Contenta OMN	Desert Springs RPQ	Bates, Paul

The room number for each debate.

The teams on the proposition side.

The teams on the opposition side.

The judges for the debates.

Teams are usually listed by the initials of the members; last names are not necessarily in alphabetical order. You should know your partners' last names so you will be able to check the pairings to get your side and room assignment.

Note the side you will be debating and where your debate will be held. Normally, the tournament will have school maps available. Check the map to see where your room is, but do not head off just yet. You have not heard the topic announcement!

Once all students have looked at the pairings sheet (there should be several copies posted in the general meeting area), the tournament director will announce the topic. You then have twenty minutes to prepare for your debate, or thirty minutes if the topic is an impromptu. Use this time wisely. First, copy any notes that you will need. Remember that you may not use printed or pre-prepared materials or speeches in your debates; you may use only notes made at preparation time.

The preparation period is a good time to consult with your teacher or coach and your teammates. If other teams from your school will be debating on the same side, work with them to get more ideas. Ideally, you did much of your preparation beforehand, but you may be less prepared for some topics than others. This is normal. In this situation, your teacher or other people from your school such as parents or assistant coaches may be very helpful.

Make sure that you arrive in your debate room on time. Sometimes you will want to prepare in the room where you will be debating. This is fine, but remember that the proposition team customarily uses the room if they choose. If you are on the opposition, you may have to prepare in another area. Keep track of the time so that you are ready to start once the twenty minutes are up.

When you get to the room, take the appropriate seat. Most debates use the following arrangement:

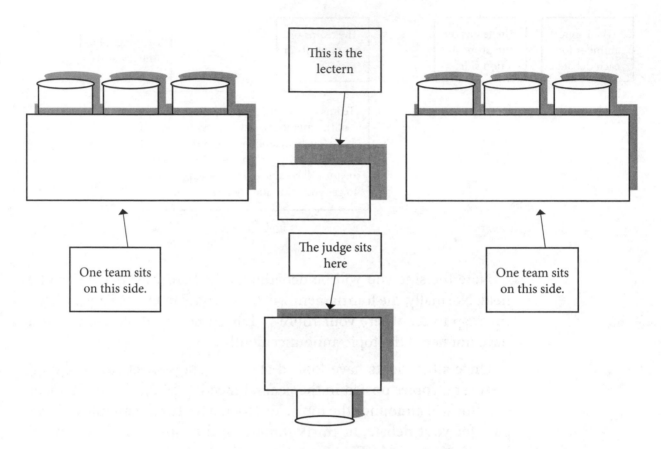

This is the lectern

One team sits on this side.

The judge sits here

One team sits on this side.

Both teams sit facing the judge, who watches them throughout the debate. Normally, there is no other audience, although parents may watch debates if they wish. Although all debaters on a team sit on the same side of the room, they do not have to sit in a specific order.

When a debate begins, the first speaker from the proposition side will stand and go to the speaking area. There may be a lectern set up for her use, or there may be simply a desk or chair on which she can put her notes. Speakers are permitted to use the notes they prepared during prep time as well as the flowsheet for the debate. In fact, the flowsheet will be very useful when you speak. It will help you organize your thoughts, respond to arguments for the other side, and extend and elaborate on arguments your teammates have presented.

As the debate progresses, different speakers will deliver their speeches and accept or refuse points of information. The judge will give hand signals showing the amount of time remaining for each speaker.

Once the debate is over, the judge will determine who has won and assign points to individual speakers. She will ask the debaters to wait outside the room while she makes her decision. After she has filled out her ballot, she will invite the debaters back into the room. Resume your seats at this time. The judge will then announce her decision and explain why she made her choice. She will also offer constructive comments to all participants. Pay careful attention to what she says and what advice she offers. This immediate feedback gives you an opportunity to improve your skills.

You must learn to win and lose debates with grace and dignity. If you have ever played a sport, a board game, or cards, you already have acquired some of these skills. Every debate is an opportunity for improvement. Debates that you do not win can be the most instructive because they encourage you to analyze your strategy and improve your skills. If you win the debate, you can still learn many things. Do not ignore the judge after she announces her decision. Listen carefully to her comments and take notes so that you can implement her suggestions in future debates and help prepare others to debate for that judge.

Do not argue with the judge. A team cannot appeal a judge's decision. The decision is final. You may disagree with her evaluation—this is normal—but part of debating involves learning to listen to and appreciate the opinions of others. If you are confused about a judge's decision, you may ask a question or two. If you still have a problem, discuss the issue with your coach.

Sometimes a debater disagrees with a judge's decision because she thought that the debate was going in a different direction than the judge did. This is the difference between communicating with yourself and communicating with another person. Communication with oneself is easier—it is more likely that you will agree with your own opinions! Convincing another person is more challenging, particularly when another team is trying to persuade the judge that you are wrong. The judge's opinions and the arguments from the opposing team interfere with the message that you are trying to communicate. It is this communication interference that leads to different perceptions about what happened in a debate.

What can you do to get more judges to vote for your side? You can pay attention to how other people perceive your points and adapt your style and content to make your speeches more persuasive. Although judges go through a training process, they still may not agree with each other about any given debate. Judging is more of an art than a science because people see issues differently. You see this in life as well as in debate. Do you agree with everyone you know on what is the best music? How about the best television program? Does everyone you know have the same political opinions? Of course not.

Judges evaluate a debate based on the arguments presented, not their own opinions or knowledge. They must consider the ideas both sides present. Remember that the judge's decision is not about which side is right or wrong, but which offered the best arguments. Your side may be right, but could still lose the debate based on the arguments made.

Return to the main gathering area for the tournament after the judge has offered her comments. The second round of debate is about to begin. You will take the other side in this debate. If you were on the proposition side in the first round, you will be on the opposition side in the second. Consult the pairing sheet and wait for the topic announcement.

Depending on the size and location of your tournament, you may have from two to six debates in a one-day event. Normally the number is either four or five. You will break for lunch, when you can eat what you brought with you or buy food from the host school's debate club boosters. The debates will become more difficult as the day progresses because the debaters are improving. Also, after the first two debates, which are paired randomly, the tournament director will pair teams against those of similar abilities. If you won your first three debates, you will face a team that has also won its first three.

At the end of the tournament, everyone gathers for the awards ceremony. This is an opportunity to celebrate the event and your participation. The tournament director and the host school will distribute trophies, medals, and other awards at this time. Usually three types of awards are given, for:

- team performance,
- individual performance,
- school performance.

At the end of the competition, the tournament director accumulates the results of the event and determines who will receive awards. Team awards go to those with a winning record (at a five-round tournament, this would be a record of three wins and two losses or better). The tournament director ranks these teams according to total wins and then by total speaker points. For example, at the end of a competition, the top five teams might be ranked in this way:

Team	Number of Wins	Total Points
Cleveland Middle RRT	5	415.5
Coombs Middle CLZ	5	415
Pioneer Middle AGS	4	416
Northview Inter. HAB	4	412.5
Parent Middle MHH	4	410

In this example, the team of Cleveland Middle School RRT would receive first place because they had the most number of wins and highest number of total points. (The total number of wins creates a tie for first place based on the team record. The tiebreaker is the total number of points for each team. In this case, Cleveland Middle RRT has 5 wins and 415.5 points, which is 0.5 points more than the Coombs Middle CLZ, which also had five wins but 415 points.)

Speaker awards go to students for their individual performances. The tournament staff totals up students' points from each debate, and the students with the most points receive awards. Normally, the top 15 to 20 percent of the participants receive them. Judges vary when assigning speaker points, but the following scale serves as a model:

- 30: Almost no one should get a 30. A perfect score should happen every few years with a really brilliant speech.

- 28-29: Brilliant.

- 26-27: Strong, well above average.

- 25: Above average.

- 23-24: Modest success as a debater.

- Points below 23 should be reserved for people who are both unsuccessful as debaters and obnoxious and mean-spirited.

- Judges may assign half-points (27.5, 25.5, etc.)

The third type of award goes to schools for overall performance, such as total number or percentage of wins.

The tournament director may also hand out certificates to all students who participated in a competition. These certificates, recognizing the considerable effort of each student contestant, are usually mailed to the participating school in the week following the tournament. In addition, tournament hosts and debate leagues may present certificates to parents and community members who earned their certification as judges. These people deserve special applause because they have demonstrated a commitment to help all students in the league continue to participate in debate and improve their abilities.

AFTER THE TOURNAMENT

After the tournament is over, reflect on your experience and develop a plan to improve your performance. Save all your notes, including your flowsheets, so that you can review them with your teammates. During the week after the tournament, you will receive copies of the ballots from your debates. These will include a detailed explanation of the judge's decision as well as his comments for debaters. Study them and compare the judges' impressions with your own. For each debate, think of at least two things your team could have done better. Develop a strategy for improving your performance at the next tournament.

If more than one team from your school attended the tournament, study their ballots for ideas and suggestions. Talk to your coaches about the debates they judged to learn what clever arguments they heard or mistakes others made that you should avoid. Finally, consider reworking speeches from the tournament using your notes and flowcharts. If a speech you gave could be improved, work on it until it is better. Ask members of your family to listen to your speech, or practice speaking in front of a mirror.

SECTION IV
APPENDICES

ISSUE ANALYSIS FORM

NAME:_____

TOPIC:_____

DATE:_____

What do I already know about this issue?

What don't I know about this issue?

Who is affected by this issue? How might they be affected?

Why is this issue important?

APPENDIX II:
DEBATE RESOURCES ON THE WEB

THE MIDDLE SCHOOL PUBLIC DEBATE PROGRAM

http://www.middleschooldebate.com

The Web site of the Middle School Public Debate Program. Here you will find expanded information in support of this text, including a free teachers' guide and program, sample debates, and issue briefs to prepare teachers and students for debate. The site also can help you find partner schools and competitions near you.

DEBATE CENTRAL

http://debate.uvm.edu

A comprehensive site on debate formats worldwide, with information on: parliamentary debate, American policy debate, Lincoln-Douglas debate, Karl Popper debate, and a number of other formats. The site contains links to debating listservs, national debate organizations, and individual debate programs. It also includes a video lecture series on parliamentary (American and British formats) and policy (American format for high school and college) debating as well as sample video debates.

INTERNATIONAL DEBATE EDUCATION ASSOCIATION

http://www.idebate.org

The virtual home of the International Debate Education Association (IDEA), an international not-for-profit organization sponsoring debate and youth education programs. The site unites more than 70,000 secondary school and college teachers and students from 27 countries.

It includes information on debating practice (primarily the Karl Popper format), youth democracy promotion and civic education, language training, and critical communication skills. The site features *Debatabase*, a searchable argument database of political, philosophical, economic, social, and cultural topics.

The Web site contains information on IDEA's international conferences and publications, member tournaments and workshops, listservs, and resources for teachers and students. Much of the material is available in English and Russian.

APPENDIX III:

THE MIDDLE SCHOOL PUBLIC DEBATE PROGRAM
JUDGING MANUAL

TABLE OF CONTENTS

INTRODUCTION TO DEBATE

This manual introduces you to the rules and procedures for judging MSPDP debates. By volunteering to serve as a judge, you are agreeing to participate in an exciting educational event. Students work very hard to prepare for contest debating. They learn teamwork, public speaking, research, argumentation, and refutation. Your role as a judge is to listen and take careful notes as the students make their points and answer the arguments from the other side. Once you have read this manual, you may become certified as a judge. For certification, you will have to participate in a training session, judge a debate with another certified judge, and then judge on your own. When you have completed these steps, you will receive a judging certificate and be eligible to judge at any MSPDP events.

In the MSPDP format, each debate has a different topic, known as the *motion* for debate. Once the motion for the debate is announced, debaters have twenty minutes to prepare their arguments. For some debates on impromptu topics, students will have thirty minutes of preparation time. This twenty or thirty minute period is known as *preparation time*, or *prep time*. Before the topic is made public, pairings are posted in the area the tournament uses for administration and collective announcements. The pairings tell teams which side they will represent, where they will debate, and who their judge will be. A pairing sheet might look like this:

Claremont McKenna Invitational, Round 3—Topic Announcement at 1:30 PM

Room	Proposition	Opposition	Judge
1	Desert Springs ABC	Frisbie DEF	B. Walters
2	Townsend GHI	Canyon Hills JKL	K. Couric
3	La Contenta MNO	Northview PQR	T. Brokaw
4	Nicolet STU	Eliot VWX	P. Jennings

Once you find your name on a pairing, collect your ballot from a tournament administrator. The ballot is your primary means of evaluating the debate you will judge.

As you can tell from the sample pairing above, there are two sides in every debate. One team is called the *proposition team*. They argue for their interpretation of a topic. To win the debate, this team needs to make and prove a case for the motion. They do not have to defend that the motion is true in all cases; they just have to prove the case is more likely true than false and sustain it successfully against opposition attacks. The other team is called the *opposition*. As their name suggests, they oppose the proposition's case. To win, this team must disprove the case the proposition makes for the motion.

Each team is composed of three debaters, each of which gives one speech. The first four speeches are *constructive* speeches. In these, debaters develop their arguments while refuting those of the other side. The last two speeches are rebuttal speeches. These are each team's final chance to show why their side should win the debate. These speeches should continue the process of refutation. The best rebuttal speakers deal with all the arguments made during the debate and show why the balance of the arguments means that their side is the winner.

The order of the speeches is as follows:

First Proposition Constructive	5 minutes
First Opposition Constructive	5 minutes
Second Proposition Constructive	5 minutes
Second Opposition Constructive	5 minutes
Opposition Rebuttal	3 minutes
Proposition Rebuttal	3 minutes

POINTS OF INFORMATION

One of the unique features of MSPDP debating is the use of *points of information*. A point of information (POI) is a request to the speaker who holds the floor to yield some of her time for a point by the opposing team. Debaters must apply for points of information. They usually do this by rising and, perhaps, extending a hand; or rising and saying "point of information," "on that point," or "information, please."

The speaker may then choose to accept or reject the application. If she does not want to take the point, she says "No, thank you." The person applying for a POI then must sit down because she does not have the floor. If the speaker accepts the point, she may say, "Yes, I'll take your point," or "Your point?" or just "Yes?"

Once the speaker has accepted a POI, the person making the point has fifteen seconds to ask her question or make a statement. She then must sit down. Note that the speaking time of the debater with the floor continues during the point of information.

Each side may attempt as many POIs as they wish. Also, there are no rules about the minimum or maximum number of points a speaker must accept during her presentation.

As a judge, you must remember two rules about POIs:

- Points of information are permitted only in the constructive speeches.

- In the constructive speeches, points of information are permitted only in the middle three minutes of each speech. The first and last minutes of each speech are *protected time*, and debaters may not make POIs during this period.

HECKLING

The Middle School Public Debate Program permits heckling. Done well, heckling improves debates by increasing interaction among participants and making the debate more dynamic. Debaters may use positive heckles. They may, for example, knock on the table or say, "hear, hear" to signify their support for an argument. They should use positive heckles judiciously and avoid disruptive behavior. If they are unruly, you may deduct speaker points from their total (more on speaker points later).

Debaters may also use negative heckles, although they should use them with extreme care. For example, they may say "shame" in a low voice to signify their strong feeling that a speaker has misrepresented one of their arguments. Debaters should not use negative heckles when they simply disagree with a speaker. That is why we have debates, after all!

REFUTATION AND THE IMPORTANCE OF CLASH

Good debates have an abundance of clash between arguments and opposing sides. Debaters cannot merely deliver impassioned speeches in support of their side. They also must directly refute the other team's arguments and justify why the key arguments sustained by their own side win them the debate.

Debaters address their opponents' arguments by using a simple four-step refutation:

1. "They say..." (briefly repeats the argument of the other side)
2. "But we disagree..." (answers the argument of the other side)
3. "Because..." (gives a reason for her disagreement or counter-argument)
4. "Therefore...." (explains what the consequence of winning this argument is)

Good debaters clash as arguments develop and evolve in response to each team's case. They must engage the arguments of the other side throughout the debate if they hope to win.

ARGUMENT EXTENSION

Debaters must not only refute the arguments of the other side but also extend their own. Argument extension is the process of subsequent speakers developing an argument. Say that the first opposition constructive speaker makes the argument that the proposed plan will cripple the economy. Argument extension occurs when the second constructive speaker answers the objections to the original argument and develops the argument further.

Debaters should extend their teammates' arguments, although they may also make new arguments to prove their side. However, they may not introduce new arguments in the rebuttal speeches (see "New Arguments" below).

In good debates, arguments grow through the process of extension. Debaters answer the objections from the other side and use those objections as springboards to flesh out their side's position.

USE OF EVIDENCE IN DEBATES

The MSPDP encourages participants to use evidence because it is critical to making a good argument. One of the skills we teach debaters is gathering and organizing facts, examples, and other data to prove their points. An informed argument is based on good reasoning and is grounded in facts and experience.

Debaters may have conducted extensive research on topics and topic areas before a tournament. However, they may not use published information (dictionaries, magazines, etc.), pre-prepared speeches, or issue briefs during the debate. They may transcribe materials and use any notes or outlines they created during preparation time.

New Arguments

Debaters must not make new arguments in the rebuttals. This is a rule, but it is also a strategic concern. New arguments made in the last proposition speech are unfair to the opposition team because they do not have a subsequent opportunity to answer them.

What is a new argument? If an argument has a foundation in the constructives, it is not a new argument. If a rebuttal speaker answers an argument, his response is not a new argument. A new argument is an entirely new line of reasoning, without any foundation in the constructive speeches, which is presented in the rebuttal speeches. If one of the opening speakers presents an argument that is abandoned until the rebuttal speeches, raising it again is considered a new argument.

What should you do when you hear a new argument in the rebuttal speeches? Note that it is new and do not let the argument factor into your decision.

JUDGING A DEBATE

INTRODUCTION TO JUDGING

One element that distinguishes debate from mere argument is that in debate two parties attempt to persuade a third, the judge. In competitive debates, the judge decides who wins. She also assigns a range of points to individual debaters.

After the debate, the judge tells the debaters how she voted and why. She also explains her decision on a paper ballot. These ballots are distributed to the participating teams and their coaches at the conclusion of the tournament or by mail in the following week.

There are as many ways of judging debates as there are ways of debating. Judges should cultivate their own styles and work with debaters to create a learning community that benefits everyone.

THE FINE ART OF JUDGING

When you judge a debate, you must decide which team wins and why. Remember that the team that wins the debate may not always be the generally better debate team. Instead, they were the better debate team in the debate that you watched. Even world-class debate teams have critical slip-ups every now and again. You must be fair and judge each debate on its own merits rather than on speculation, past performance, or other factors.

Judging debates can be intimidating. You may feel unprepared or inexperienced, especially compared to the debaters. In reality, no matter what your experience level, you are prepared to judge a debate. Even if you have never seen a debate before, you can still render a thoughtful and informed decision based only on your engaged participation. Middle school debates are meant to be entertaining and accessible to judges and audiences of all experience levels, so even if you are a novice, you will fit in. The certification process and judge trainers will help you get used to what is involved with judging. You will also improve as you watch and judge more debates. You have to start somewhere, so do not be intimidated. All you have to do is make the best decision you can.

Everyone recognizes, though, that some decisions are better than others. Judges hold opinions. This is normal, healthy, and in the interest of building lively communities. There is, however, a difference between having opinions and forcing them on others at the expense of reasoned debate and discussion. Judges should maintain an open mind about the arguments and the examples used as evidence. Open-mindedness is not so much an issue of surrendering convictions as it is of respecting the debaters' opinions and efforts. Remember that middle school debate is switch-side debating. Students do not get to choose their side in any given debate. On occasion, you may have the opportunity to watch debaters defending a side contrary to what they (or you) might otherwise agree with. This is why it is especially important to be fair and unbiased when deciding debates.

BE OPEN-MINDED AND FAIR TO BOTH TEAMS.

What do we mean when we say that some decisions are better than others are? A good decision is one that relies on a consistent, fair method of deliberation. In order to judge fairly, you must keep a few things in mind:

- *Identify your biases* and resist them.

- *Apply reciprocal standards* for evaluating arguments. Do not hold an error against one team and ignore it when the other team makes it. Make your judging standards relevant and apply them fairly to all debate participants.

- *Presume that the debaters are acting in good faith*. Resist the temptation to read intention into debaters' mistakes. A debater may not know that he made a factual error. Do not assume that he is being deceitful.

- *Be patient.* During the course of a debate, the participants may do many things that irritate you. They probably are not doing them on purpose.

- *Give debaters the benefit of the doubt about their choices.* They may not make the choices you would, but that is okay.

Debates offer bright critical thinkers an opportunity to imagine, analyze, and innovate. If you do not give them the benefit of the doubt, you could stifle their creativity or substitute your vision for theirs.

- ***Do not pre-interpret the topic.*** The debaters interpret the topic. Do not impose your opinion. How they interpret the topic is not relevant to the outcome of the debate.

Good decisions are reached fairly with appropriate and adequate deliberation on the issues and arguments presented. Good judges know and follow the rules of the particular format and tournament.

How should you conduct yourself during a debate? We have told debaters that they should not treat the judge as if she were a passive info-receptacle propped up at the back of the room with a pen and a ballot. Just as the debaters should conduct themselves appropriately toward you, so you should act appropriately toward them. The following is a list of "Don'ts" for aspiring and experienced judges:

- Don't discuss how the debate is going during the debate. Your role is nonverbal until after the debate is finished.

- Don't penalize debaters who speak in accents other than your own. Take into consideration that, for some, English may not be their native tongue.

- Don't usurp the role of the judge for personal whim (e.g., "You must use the words 'x, y, z' in the course of your speeches"; "Tell a joke and I will give you thirty points"). The course and content of the debate is not yours to dictate.

- Don't arbitrarily manufacture rules (e.g., "Points of information must be in the form of a question"; "New *examples* are prohibited in the rebuttal speeches").

- Don't write the ballot during the rebuttal speeches. This practice conveys a disregard for the competitors and for the integrity of the process. Wait until after the debate to make your decision and fill in the ballot.

- Don't ignore the rules to suit your own preferences.

- Don't use marginalizing and discriminatory rhetoric or practice (anti-Semitic commentary; sexual harassment; voting against participants for fashion, hairstyle, body piercings, etc.). This rule should be obvious.

This list may seem long, but you can summarize it in one sentence: *Be respectful of the debaters and be fair and professional in your conduct and evaluation of the debate.*

What to Bring to a Debate

- *Paper and a pen*
- *A timing device (stopwatch, kitchen timer, or watch with a second hand)*

Always bring paper and pen to the debate. We encourage you to flow the debate, i.e., take notes in the form adapted specifically to debating. (There is a sample flowsheet below). Many complex arguments are exchanged and refuted during the course of a debate, and you will need notes to follow and assess them. No matter how reliable your memory, if you do not take notes, you risk missing a crucial example or answer. Good note taking always helps you decide who wins and explains your decision. Note taking also indicates to the debaters your seriousness of purpose.

As judge, you are responsible for timing the debate. You will have to give time signals to debaters during their speeches. The most important signal tells debaters when protected time begins and ends. In the previous section, we explained that protected time is the first and last minute of each constructive speech. Signal the end of the first minute by slapping the table in an audible fashion so that debaters know they can now attempt points of information. Similarly, slap the table when the last minute of the constructive has begun so that debaters know that POIs are out of order.

The easiest way to give time signals is with your hands. Raise three fingers when the speaker has three minutes remaining, two fingers when the speaker has two minutes remaining, and so forth. Use a half-bent single finger to indicate that 30 seconds remain in a speech. When time is up, hold up a fist to show that the debater must stop.

Getting to the Point: Deciding Who Wins and Why

How do you determine who wins the debate? You base your decision on the criteria the debaters offered. Every debate is about different issues, is conducted differently, and thus should be decided on its own merits. Different teams will offer different kinds of arguments. You must decide whether the proposition team has made a case for endorsing the debate motion. The opposition team will make arguments about why the proposition's case is inadequate, dangerous, or otherwise misguided. You will have to evaluate the merits of these arguments and decide whether the proposition team's rejoinders are satisfactory.

During the course of the debate, the participants may offer different criteria for your decision. They may even address you directly, saying that your vote should or should not be based on a particular argument or set of arguments. They are not trying to order you around; rather, they are hoping to influence your decision.

Do not decide the debate based simply on the number of arguments won by each side. You also must evaluate the qualitative significance of each argument. Take this common scenario: The proposition wins an advantage conclusively, while the opposition wins a disadvantage conclusively. Who wins? You cannot decide based on the information we have given you. You need to know the relative significance of the advantage and disadvantage. This relative significance can have both quantitative and qualitative aspects. You may be tempted to decide based simply on the biggest impact. For example, you may decide to vote for the proposition team because they claimed to avert a war, while the opposition team was able to prove only that the proposition's proposal would cause the deaths of hundreds of children.

But impact is only one element affecting your decision; you also must consider questions of risk and probability. In the above example, your decision would doubtless change if there were a very low probability that the proposition's plan would avert a war. Do not interject your own risk calculation at this point. The debaters may have weighed the round for you. That is, they may have made the best case as to why their arguments are more important than or more instrumental to the decision than those of the other team. If the debaters do compare arguments, you need to take these comparisons into account.

Judges frequently make the mistake of voting for the opposition team on the basis of partial arguments. A partial argument is one in which the opposition team says that the proposition's case will not solve the problem completely, or that the problem is not quite as bad as the proposition team claims. These are good defensive arguments for the opposition team, but they should almost never be reasons to vote for the opposition. These arguments prove only that the proposition case is not as good as claimed. Big deal. Rarely are the arguments concluded in debates as triumphant as predicted. The proposition team can still win if they show their case to be comparatively advantageous; that is, if they can show that it is better by some increment than the present state of affairs.

Do not vote based on your personal opinions. You may have strong views about the topic. Perhaps you are a committed opponent of the death penalty and have to judge a debate on this subject. You may find that your personal presumption lies with the team that opposes the death penalty, but do not hold the other team to a higher burden of proof. The teams do not have to persuade you personally of the correctness of their position; the debaters are debating each other, not you.

Track arguments as they develop so that you can assess the debate in the fairest way possible. Some new judges decide the debate solely on the quality of the final rebuttal speech. This is a mistake because the proposition rebuttal should be evaluated both as a response to the opposition's arguments and as a summation of the proposition team's final position. When deciding the debate, you must determine if the proposition rebuttalist dropped or failed to answer any opposition arguments. You must then determine how to weigh the conceded arguments in the context of the other arguments in the debate.

Some conceded arguments will not affect your decision, others will. If an argument is conceded, you must assign the full weight of that argument to the side that argued it. Nevertheless, a team does not automatically lose the debate if it concedes some arguments. All arguments are not equal. You must evaluate the conceded and disputed arguments to decide if the proposition team has proven their case given the balance of arguments in the debate.

Some arguments may be introduced, only to have the team that introduced them later yield to the other team on their original claim. This is smart debating. Opposition teams frequently present a wider variety of arguments in their first speech than in their subsequent ones. This tactic is called argument selection and is good debate practice. Do not penalize teams for not extending all of their arguments through the entire debate.

FILLING OUT YOUR BALLOT

SPEAKER POINTS

In addition to deciding which team wins the debate, you must fill out your ballot and assign points to each speaker. Speaker points are a measure of individual performance. Most tournaments give speaker awards based on a speaker's aggregate point accumulation during the tournament. Usually, you will rank the debaters on a thirty-point scale. The team that wins the debate is not necessarily the team that gets the highest speaker points. The total number of points does not decide who wins the debate.

We suggest the following guidelines for assigning points:

For a thirty-point scale:

- 30: Almost no one should get a 30. A perfect score should happen every few years with a really brilliant speech.

- 28-29: Brilliant

- 26-27: Strong, well above average

- 25: Above average

- 23-24: Modest success as a debater

- Reserve points below 23 for people who are both unsuccessful as debaters and also obnoxious and mean-spirited.

- Never drop points below a 20, even if a debater was particularly bad. Lower points frequently exclude a debate team from elimination rounds; so if you give points below 20, you are saying that a debater has no chance of rehabilitation in any other debates.

- You may assign half-points (27.5, 25.5, etc.).

After assigning points and ranking the debaters, you must write your ballot. Use the space provided on the ballot to explain your decision. Why did you vote the way you did? What arguments were most persuasive? Why? Give advice and constructive criticism to the debaters. What did they do well? How could they improve their performance or their arguments? Use as much of the ballot space as possible. Debaters and their coaches save ballots and often use them as references and resources. You also should deliver an oral critique, however brief, to the teams you judge. Whatever interaction you have with the debaters immediately after the debate will be more valuable than your written comments.

TAKING NOTES IN DEBATES

USING THE SAMPLE FLOWSHEET

Taking notes in debates is called flowing. At the end of this manual, you will find a sample flowsheet from part of a hypothetical debate about school uniforms. Note that the flowsheet is divided into columns. Each column is labeled for a speech (or speeches—more on that in just a second): "1PC" is the first proposition constructive, "1OC" is the first opposition constructive, "2PC" is the second proposition constructive, "2OC" is the second opposition constructive, "OR" is the opposition rebuttal, and "PR" is the proposition rebuttal. "2OC" and "OR" are in the same column because the speeches are back to back and function as a unified front for the opposition.

Students and judges use each column to track arguments made in that speech. Say the proposition team makes a brief case for student uniforms. They might advance three basic arguments:

- Cost: Uniforms are cheaper than fashionable clothes. Many students cannot afford to look sharp every day for school, and students are embarrassed if they do not have the latest fashions.

- Distraction: Uniforms are not as distracting as the current fashions and will help students focus on their class work, not their clothes.

- Violence: Mandating uniforms reduces violence because it prevents students from wearing gang clothes or gang symbols.

As the first proposition speaker makes her case, both you and the other debaters should take notes on your flowsheets.

The first opposition speaker then refutes the case. She might introduce the issue of freedom of expression. She could say that uniforms are a bad idea because students need to express their individuality in school. Then she would answer the arguments made in the proposition's case. On the cost point, she might say that uniforms are expensive, too, particularly since people have to buy several at once. On the distraction point, she might say that many things distract students, and that districts have dress codes to deal with distracting clothing. Finally, on the violence point, she might say that dress codes already forbid gang clothing, and that mandating uniforms would not reduce the gang problem because students who want to join gangs will do so regardless of the policy.

The second proposition speaker must then answer the opposition's arguments while rebuilding and extending the proposition's case. The flowsheet will help her do this because she knows what arguments she has to answer and extend. She should begin by answering the freedom of expression argument by saying, for example, that students have many ways to express themselves, and that clothing is a shallow and unimportant method of expression. Then she should move on to rebuild her team's case. To extend the cost argument, she should reiterate it briefly before beginning her refutation: "We said that many students cannot afford to keep up with the latest trends, and that's embarrassing. Now, they said that uniforms are expensive, but they are cheap compared to the latest pair of Nikes or Hilfigers, and that means that poorer students won't be made fun of for their clothes." She could repeat this process with the other arguments

You see how this process works. Arguments are refuted, extended, and compared through the debate. Every speech, therefore, has a rebuttal component. Teams may introduce new arguments as well, but only in the constructive speeches.

SAMPLE FLOWSHEET

1st Proposition Const.	1st Opposition Const.	2nd Proposition Const.	2nd Opp/Opp Rebuttal	Proposition Rebuttal
Students should have uniforms.	Hurts freedom of expression—students need to express individuality.	1. Students have other ways to express themselves. 2. Clothes not important for expression—too shallow.		
1. Cost—many can't afford expensive clothes; are embarrassed.	Uniforms expensive too—must buy a lot at once.	Students can't keep up with trends—Nikes. Even if uniforms expensive, clothes are worse. Also, poor students won't be made fun of.		
2. Not as distracting, so students can focus on class work.	1. Always things to distract students. 2. Dress codes address the problem.			
3. Reduce violence—students can't wear gang symbols or clothes.	1. Dress codes already stop gang clothing. 2. Uniforms won't help—they join for other reasons.			

MIDDLE SCHOOL PUBLIC DEBATE PROGRAM SAMPLE BALLOT

Round:_____ Location:_____

Judge's Name:_____

****please Rank Debaters On A Scale Of 1—30 Points.****

Proposition Team:_____ | Opposition Team:_____

1st:_____ points:___ | 1st:_____ points:___

2nd:_____ points:___ | 2nd:_____ points:___

3rd:_____ points:___ | 3rd:_____points:___

IN MY OPINION, THE TEAM THAT WON THE DEBATE WAS THE (CIRCLE ONE) PROP / OPP.

SIGNATURE:_____

AFFILIATION:_____

Please use the space below to indicate the reasons for your decision and to provide helpful comments to the debaters.

APPENDIX IV:
TIPS FOR JUDGES

Don't forget!

You're responsible for timing the debate.

Signal the beginning and end of protected time.

Reveal your decision after the debate with comments for debaters.

MIDDLE SCHOOL PUBLIC DEBATE PROGRAM

Sponsored by Claremont McKenna College

Things to Remember When Judging

LEAVE YOUR OPINIONS AT THE DOOR! The only facts known in the debate are what the teams bring forth. It is not the job of a 13-year-old to change a judge's lifelong belief.

DON'T FILL IN FOR SPEAKERS. Judges should not "fill in" what they believe a speaker was going to say, should have said, or probably meant. What speakers say is what the speakers said, and that's all there is.

PROPOSITION TEAMS MAY REASONABLY "SHRINK" A TOPIC. But defining a topic is restricted to defining words in the topic within reasonable limits, such as a "child" being defined as between the ages of eight and sixteen, rather than a "child" being defined as a juvenile cactus clinging to the nether regions of the Arabian Peninsula.

TAKE THOROUGH NOTES ON YOUR FLOWSHEET. This will help you decide the debate and set a good example for the students.

Order of Speeches & Time

First Proposition Constructive --5

First Opposition Constructive --5

Second Proposition Constructive --5

Second Opposition Constructive --5

Opposition Rebuttal --3

Proposition Rebuttal --3

ASSIGNING SPEAKER POINTS

You will have to assign points to all students in the debate. These points are a measure of individual performance in the debate. We suggest you use the following scale:

- 30: Almost no one should get a 30. A perfect score should happen every few years with a really brilliant speech.
- 28-29: Brilliant
- 26-27: Strong, well above average
- 25: Above average
- 23-24: Modest success as a debater
- Points below 23 should be reserved for people who are both unsuccessful as debaters and are also obnoxious and mean-spirited.
- Points should never drop below a 20, even if a debater was particularly bad. Lower points frequently exclude a debate team from elimination rounds; so if you give points below 20, you are saying that a debater has no chance of rehabilitation in any other debates.

You may assign half-points (27.5, 25.5, etc.).

SAMPLE TOPICS FOR DEBATE

All the topics below have been used in national and international tournament competitions over the past several years. This list is an effective tool for teaching and practice. Debaters can use the topics for preparation: Pick a few topics at a time and generate case ideas and topic interpretations for each, linking the case to the motion. Teachers, trainers, and coaches can use the list to provide practice topics for their students. They may also use the topics in tournaments or other kinds of scrimmages among debaters or debate squads. The most important function of this list, however, is to show the wide range of debate topics.

CRIMINAL JUSTICE

The United States should ban the death penalty.

California should eliminate its "three strikes" law.

Defendants should be required to testify at their own trials.

The United States should abolish the jury system.

This House prefers rehabilitation to retribution.

Electing judges is better than appointing them.

This House would televise criminal trials.

Violent juvenile offenders ought to be treated as adults in the criminal justice system.

Communities should have tougher punishments for graffiti.

The United States should reduce punishments for "victimless crimes."

ECONOMICS AND FISCAL POLICY

California should substantially increase the minimum wage.

The United States should pay reparations for slavery.

Wealthy people's taxes should be raised and poor people's taxes lowered.

The government should increase "sin" taxes.

The federal budget deficit is good for America.

The government should subsidize some businesses and farms.

All employees should have the right to strike.

The work week should be shortened to thirty hours.

This House would end corporate welfare.

The federal government should establish a national public works program for the unemployed.

The federal government should significantly curtail the powers of labor unions.

This House would set a maximum limit on salaries.

EDUCATION AND SCHOOL POLICY

Cellular phones should be allowed in schools.

Junk food should be banned in schools.

School should be year-round.

All middle schools should require student uniforms.

Schools should use filtering software to prevent children from viewing restricted material on the Internet.

Middle schools should increase required classes and reduce electives.

Schools should not use standardized testing.

The Supreme Court should end affirmative action in higher education.

Schools should not support competitive interscholastic sports.

There should be mandatory drug testing for participation in extracurricular activities.

Schools should ban animal dissection.

Advertising in public schools does more good than harm.

College athletes should be paid.

The No Child Left Behind Act has done more good than harm.

High school students should have to pass a national exit exam to graduate.

Middle schools should allow outside food vendors to supply lunch.

School attendance should be voluntary.

Schools should eliminate letter grades.

The United States should guarantee a free college education to all citizens.

Vocational training is more important than liberal arts education.

Charter schools do more harm than good.

Teachers' salaries should be based on students' academic performance.

ENVIRONMENTAL POLICY

The United States should open federal lands and offshore areas for oil drilling.

The United States should adopt a new timber policy.

The United States should ratify the Kyoto Accord.

This House would restrict private car ownership.

Economic growth is more important than environmental protection.

High oil prices do more good than harm.

This House would act decisively to stop global warming.

The government should substantially reduce oil imports.

HEALTH

Cigarettes should be illegal.

This House believes that good health is a human right.

This House would hold tobacco companies liable for the consequences of their products.

The government should provide universal health care.

IMMIGRATION AND IMMIGRANTS

California should issue drivers' licenses to undocumented immigrants.

The United States should adopt English as the official national language.

The United States should allow peaceful and healthy immigrants to cross the border freely.

The United States should not restrict immigration.

Resident non-citizens should have the right to vote.

INDIVIDUAL RIGHTS AND CIVIL LIBERTIES

The free press does more good than harm.

The government should adopt a policy of mandatory background checks for the purchasers of firearms.

Possession of handguns should be made illegal.

Gun manufacturers should be held liable for gun-related deaths.

The Constitution should contain a right to privacy.

All hate speech should be banned.

A journalist's right to shield confidential sources ought to be protected by the First Amendment.

California should end all classification by race.

The right to privacy is more important than the freedom of the press.

The United States should adopt a National Identification Card.

The government should legalize voluntary euthanasia.

Children should have a mandatory curfew.

This House would ban smoking in public places.

The protection of public safety justifies random drug testing.

Torture is justified for national security.

People who want to have children should be required to obtain a license.

Homeland security is more important than the protection of civil liberties.

The United States should have a draft for military service.

California should raise the minimum driving age to eighteen.

INTERNATIONAL AFFAIRS

The U.S. invasion of Iraq has done more harm than good.

The United States should eliminate its own weapons of mass destruction.

On balance, free trade is better than fair trade.

Saudi Arabia is more an enemy than an ally of the United States.

The United States is losing the War on Terror.

NAFTA should be extended throughout the Americas.

The United States should end its embargo of Cuba.

The United Nations has failed.

The United Nations Security Council should not have veto power.

The possession of nuclear weapons is immoral.

Protection of human rights justifies the use of military force.

The United States should sign the Ottawa Treaty banning the production and export of land mines.

This House supports the establishment of an international criminal court.

It is immoral to use economic sanctions to achieve foreign policy goals.

MEDIA AND TELEVISION

This House would ban all tobacco advertising.

Television is a bad influence.

Violent video games should be banned.

The American media works against the best interests of the public.

The federal government should significantly strengthen the regulation of mass media communication.

It is proper for the government to own the TV and radio airwaves.

This House would televise executions.

This House believes that the state should have no role in broadcasting.

PHILOSOPHY AND ETHICS

This House believes that it is never right to take a life.

This House believes that the ends do not justify the means.

Eating meat is unethical.

The fact that most people believe something is good makes it good.

Housing should be a basic human right.

POLITICS

The United States should lower the voting age.

This House believes in term limits for federal officials.

The United States should have a parliamentary government.

This House believes that negative political advertising is significantly detrimental to the democratic process.

The United States should abolish the Electoral College.

This House would ban all private donations to political parties.

The District of Columbia should be granted statehood.

The United States should have more than two political parties.

The Constitution should be amended to allow non-native-born citizens to be president.

This House would use proportional representation to decide national elections.

This House would support a six-year presidential term of office.

Special interest groups have too much influence in elections.

This House would adopt a system of compulsory voting for all citizens.

Popular Culture

American culture places too great an emphasis on athletic success.

There should be integration of the sexes in professional sports.

This House supports a national lottery.

Consumers should not purchase SUVs.

Beauty pageants do more good than harm.

The United States should ban hunting for sport.

State lotteries should be ended.

The United States should abolish state funding of the arts.

Peer pressure is more beneficial than harmful.

Ban boxing!

The use of animals for public entertainment should be illegal.

Parents should not purchase war toys for their children.

Parents should be punished for their children's mistakes.

Science and Technology

The United States should significantly increase space exploration.

The United States should permit human cloning.

This House would ban all experimentation on animals.

President Bush's plan for space exploration will do more good than harm.

When in conflict, this House values scientific discovery over the welfare of animals.

The government should substantially increase the use of nuclear power.

The use of antibiotics should be significantly limited.

Genetic engineering does more harm than good.

Genetically modified foods do more good than harm.

United Kingdom

This House would tax the monarchy.

This House would give Britain a written constitution.

This House would limit the terms of MPs.

Resolved: That the Government should adopt a program of compulsory health insurance for all citizens.

This House would allow eighteen-year-olds to be MPs.

This House would introduce proportional representation in Britain.

This House believes that the "first past the post" system is undemocratic.

This House would privatize the BBC.

Britain has failed in its responsibilities to refugees.

The NHS should be privatized.

This House would abolish the Commonwealth.

This House would dissolve the House of Lords.

The A-level does more harm than good.

U.S. History

This House would remain loyal to King George III.

For securing individual rights, the central government is better than local governments.

This House would support U.S. isolationism.

An enlightened monarch is preferable to a chaotic legislature.

This House would not sign the Articles of Confederation.

Political compromise undermined the ideals of the American Revolution.

U.S. westward expansion was justified.

The principal of judicial review established in *Marbury* v. *Madison* has gone too far.

Majority rule does not protect the rights of minorities.

This House would join Shays's Rebellion.

This House regrets the Monroe Doctrine.

The U.S. government should not support privateering.

The spoils system is necessary for government.

This House would not have gone to war with Mexico.

In this [fill in the blank] case, the United States should break a treaty.

This House would not vote for Andrew Jackson.

This House would choose gold over silver.

Texas should remain an independent nation.

The North should have let the South secede.

The cotton gin has done more harm than good.

Conscription is immoral.

The Draft Riots were justified.

The South should supervise its own reconstruction.

A war crimes court should be established for civil war veterans.

Laissez-faire economics do more harm than good.

Urbanization produces misery.

World History

Mesopotamia was a greater influence on world history than Egypt.

This House would follow Hammurabi's code.

Athenian democracy is better than representative democracy.

The advancement of civilization through empire did more good than harm.

The caste system was good for Indian society.

When in conflict, Confucianism is better than Taoism.

The invention of gunpowder did more good than harm.